MISS MAGGIE'S
KITCHEN

For Gabin & Balthazar

Design: Florence Cailly and Claude-Olivier Four
Editorial Director: Florence Lécuyer
Editor: Clélia Ozier-Lafontaine

English Edition
Editorial Director: Kate Mascaro
Editor: Helen Adedotun
Translated from the French by Ansley Evans
Copyediting: Wendy Sweetser
Typesetting: Claude-Olivier Four
Proofreading: Kate van den Boogert
Production: Titouan Roland
Color Separation: IGS-CP, L'Isle d'Espagnac
Printed in Bosnia and Herzegovina by GPS

Originally published in French as *Chez Miss Maggie's Kitchen*
© Flammarion. S.A., Paris. 2019

English-language edition
© Flammarion. S.A., Paris. 2020

editions.flammarion.com

20 21 22   3 2 1

ISBN: 978-2-08-020445-5

Legal Deposit: 04/2020

HÉLOÏSE BRION

MISS MAGGIE'S
—— KITCHEN ——
Relaxed French Entertaining

Photography by
CHRISTOPHE ROUÉ

Flammarion

CONTENTS

INTRODUCTION

I grew up between two countries: the United States and France. Throughout each school year in Florida, life followed the rhythm of regular holidays and celebrations like Thanksgiving, Easter, and birthdays. For these festive events, my mother and I would decorate our home with care to fit the occasion. During my summer vacations in France, the rhythm shifted, and daily family meals in the French tradition set the pace of each passing day. In our family's old mountain farmhouse tucked away in the Pyrenees, spontaneity was the norm. Between friends passing through, neighbors from nearby villages dropping by, and lost hikers, it was not unusual to find twenty of us gathered around the table. Every meal was a party! With no electricity, we cooked over an open wood fire, and everyone took part in preparing the meals. We would source our ingredients locally, like the best peaches and tomatoes from a local farmer friend and goat cheese from a farmhouse on the mountain opposite our home. Memories from these summer days are deeply etched in my mind—the fragrant bread, peach-apricot jam bubbling away over the flames, honey from my great-grandfather's hives, vintage hand-embroidered table linens, candlelight, crackling fires, and all the dishes we made together, with their indelible aromas and flavors.

In 2015, when I was pregnant with my second son, my husband and I fell in love with an old hunting lodge in Normandy with a distinctly British look. We purchased the lodge and christened it "Miss Maggie." I had always loved cooking and having people over, but this house was a real turning point for me, and a true source of inspiration. In the fall of 2016—the year I turned forty and after fifteen years in the fashion industry—I sensed the need for a change. I wanted to expand my horizons and feel more fulfilled. So Christophe, my husband, encouraged me to self-publish a recipe journal for family and friends, who often asked me to share my culinary secrets. I published the first issue in December 2016 as a holiday gift, with the title "Miss Maggie's Kitchen" printed on the cover. Following the success of this first issue, a second—still printed in limited quantities—was published in March, for family and friends but also for a few other people who had heard about it. Requests just kept growing.

MORE THAN JUST MAKING A MEAL TO FEED OUR BODIES, COOKING IS AN ACT OF LOVE PERFORMED FOR OUR FAMILY, FRIENDS, AND GUESTS, AND THIS SHINES THROUGH IN THE FOOD WE SERVE.

and so I decided to dedicate myself more fully to Miss Maggie's Kitchen, launching the company and website on—coincidentally—July 4, 2017. The name has stuck, and this serendipitous project that combines all of my passions has become my main pursuit.

Since this shift, I have cherished sharing and exchanging recipes and ideas with people around the world. In this time, I have also realized that many women (I mostly hear from women) feel insecure in the kitchen. They want to cook for themselves and others but lack the self-confidence to do so. With this book, I hope to help readers overcome their doubts with highly doable recipes and table settings—it's all a question of pairing! As I am a self-taught cook myself, I want to take readers by the hand and show them that everything in this book is achievable. The most important thing is to cook with intention. According to a popular saying, "cooking is love made visible." More than just making a meal to feed our bodies, cooking is an act of love performed for our family, friends, and guests, and this shines through in the food we serve.

I do not have any set rituals or rules for the time I spend in the kitchen—it all depends on the circumstances. Sometimes I cook in silence, other times to music, and I am just as happy cooking alone as with others. I can often be found dancing in my kitchen! We must all discover what works best to brush away our fears and trust our instincts. I am certain there is a great cook within each of us. I also believe that recipes are made to be passed along, as they have been for generations, evolving in the hands of each cook. And cookbooks are made to be written in and stained with oil or spices. That's cooking! So I hope my recipes will evolve in your hands, with your own creative touch—feel free to swap out the ingredients listed for something you like better or happen to have on hand, depending on the season. Hearing from readers is one of my greatest joys. I love knowing, for instance, that guests have loved a meal, or that a family traveling around the world on a boat has adapted my recipes according to the ingredients they have found in one country or another. The chain of sharing extends far and wide.

Welcome to Miss Maggie's Kitchen!

I BELIEVE THAT FOOD
CAN NOURISH BOTH
OUR BODY AND MIND
IF WE ARE ABLE
TO IDENTIFY
WHAT WE ARE EATING.

MY PHILOSOPHY OF LIFE

Sharing is essential in my life—a favorite spot; a moment halfway around the world or at the local café; ideas and dreams; expertise; and, especially, beloved recipes and good meals. The meal is a universal shared moment. In the kitchen and around the table, we experience a wide range of emotions together with those we love; these essential life lessons make us who we are. Meals also evoke memories—a scent can catch us by surprise and remind us of an event, place, or person that had seemed buried in our minds. That is the power of food.

For me, cooking with affection for my loved ones and guests is one of the simplest and purest of actions. It is a means to express ourselves and demonstrate our love for our family, friends, and community. We are nourishing our bodies and our minds! And the kitchen, more than any other room, is a powerfully symbolic place charged with memories across cultures and generations. The site of many first tastes and smells, the kitchen is often the soul of a home, a family, or even a group of friends. It is a place where we prepare, taste, explore, and discover. Not coincidentally, it is also where people tend to gather during parties, and, more often than not, where the best time is had. Yet this room is also conducive to intimacy—far more secrets are shared in the kitchen than over a cup of tea in the living room! In today's ever-connected, hyper-consuming world, I try to slow down the clock and fully enjoy each moment with the people I love. The best place I have found for doing this is in the kitchen, around a table. Creating with my hands nourishes me, centers me, and reconnects me to my best self. I am a hands-on cook, and even if some days I dream of a beautiful stand mixer, I deeply enjoy making dough by hand and procure great pleasure from selecting and picking herbs in the garden with my bare hands. In the kitchen, I learn, fail, start over again, take risks, and surprise myself. This awakens my creativity, and I feel I have found my place, in perfect harmony.

We all have a story to tell. By sharing my world in the pages of this book, I wish to celebrate the act of cooking, and everything it can bring us and has brought us in our lives.

I CANNOT RESIST RUMMAGING THROUGH VILLAGE ANTIQUE MARKETS FOR UNIQUE FINDS—PERHAPS A PLATE OR TWO, A SERVING DISH, A CARAFE, BEAUTIFUL SILVERWARE, OR VINTAGE LINENS.

MY SOURCES OF INSPIRATION

I take inspiration from many sources: my childhood memories, nature, the seasons, local ingredients, the weekly farmers market, travels, art, and artisans. All of these things nourish me and fuel my creations, whether it be a recipe or a table setting.

MY COOKING STYLE

I like to cook everyday fare that is meant for sharing, and I am partial to recipes that everyone around the table will enjoy, all generations combined. I love preparing large family-style dishes and setting them in the center of the table, so that everyone can participate in serving. This helps create a relaxed vibe that encourages conversation and exchange. When I develop recipes, I make sure they are easily achievable, with accessible techniques and ingredients like seasonal produce and readily available condiments and spices. My cooking is decidedly unfussy with a focus on all that is fresh, seasonal, and local. It reflects my cross-cultural upbringing, with elements of the traditional French family meal and a more laid-back side from my time in the United States. I believe that food can nourish both our body and mind if we are able to identify what we are eating. When we use quality ingredients, we must honor and respect them, not transform them. Cooking is really about pairing flavors and colors, just like composing a painting. When friends drop by unexpectedly, I love inspecting the refrigerator and pantry to see what I have and figuring out how I can put it together to create a treat for them. In fact, this is how one of my signature recipes—the zucchini and burrata tart— was born.

MY DECORATING STYLE

At the table, our five senses must be nourished, and, to me, the table itself is just as important as the food on the plates. In fact, I am convinced that meals are more enjoyable and memorable if they take place around a beautiful table. When we evoke all of the senses,

I LOVE CREATING DIFFERENT AMBIANCES ACCORDING TO THE SEASON, THE PLACE, AND THE GUESTS.

we spark emotions and create lasting memories. A meal is like a story that we set in motion and then co-create with our guests. This story is a combination of the lighting, the staging, the music and laughter, the aromas from simmering pots, the feel of quality products and of the dining table—whether wooden, marble, or covered with a washed linen tablecloth—and, finally, the flavors. During a meal, we all embark on a journey together. I love creating different ambiances according to the season, the place, and the guests. People often think you have to splash out on expensive decorations to do this, but that is not the case at all! I am a fan of small details, which I use alongside treasures I find on outdoor walks. Using natural elements like flowers, branches, and seasonal fruits and vegetables, along with repurposed objects, is achievable and affordable for everyone! I love the ephemeral, evolving nature of this approach—it makes each meal truly unique! This is also a great way to spark creativity, both your own and that of those around you. My sons, for instance, love bringing me stones,

flowers, and shells for my future table settings. I, too, started gathering objects for the table at an early age. When I was a child, my parents liked to take back roads rather than highways in order to discover charming villages, little restaurants serving tasty dishes, and secondhand shops filled with treasures, where I bought the first pieces in my tableware collection. Still today, I cannot resist rummaging through village antique markets for unique finds—perhaps a plate or two, a serving dish, a carafe, beautiful silverware, or vintage linens. Beyond their aesthetic appeal, these timeworn objects hold countless stories. We can only imagine the lively meals that these glasses and plates must have participated in! I also like the fact that using secondhand objects is more eco-friendly and sustainable than buying new items for each occasion. Of course, I sometimes make exceptions, like when I fall for a gorgeous handmade ceramic dish or artisanal glassware. I love mixing these different pieces together and mismatching, to give the table a twist—a relaxed yet chic touch that pairs perfectly with my cooking!

ESSENTIALS AND BASE RECIPES

IN MY KITCHEN
I ALWAYS HAVE...

MY FAVORITE INGREDIENTS

Five-peppercorn blend
Fleur de sel
Fresh rosemary
Fresh thyme
Lemon (preferably organic)
Extra-virgin olive oil

ALLIUMS

Garlic
Onions
Scallions
Shallots

CONDIMENTS

Anchovies
Apple cider vinegar
Balsamic vinegar (traditional
and white)
Hazelnut oil
White truffle oil
Whole grain mustard

DAIRY AND EGGS

Butter (unsalted and
lightly salted)
Eggs
Parmesan

DRIED FRUITS AND NUTS

Almonds
Cranberries
Hazelnuts
Pecans
Pistachios
Pumpkin seeds

FRESH FRUITS AND VEGETABLES

Whatever is in season

GRAINS AND LEGUMES (PULSES)

Bulgur wheat
Couscous
Farro
Lentils
Pasta
Quinoa
Rice

HERBS

Basil
Chives
Lemon verbena
Oregano
Sage
Savory

PANTRY BASICS

Baking soda
Cane sugar
Chocolate
Coconut milk
Flour
Honey
Maple syrup
Orange blossom water
Yeast

SPICES

Bay leaves
Cardamom (pods and ground)
Cayenne pepper
Cinnamon (sticks and ground)
Coriander (seeds and ground)
Cumin (seeds and ground)
Fennel (seeds and ground)
Ginger
Paprika
Pepper
Quatre-épices spice mix (ginger,
nutmeg, cloves, and allspice)
Seasoned salt (e.g. with
cumin and lemon zest—
see recipe p. 26)
Star anise
Turmeric
Vanilla beans
Whole cloves
Whole nutmeg
Za'atar (see recipe p. 27)

SHORTCRUST PASTRY DOUGH

This is my go-to pastry dough, which I adapt according to the sweet or savory pie or tart I am making (see suggestions below).

ACTIVE TIME
10 minutes

CHILLING TIME
30 minutes

INGREDIENTS
2 cups (9 oz./250 g) all-purpose flour
1 pinch fleur de sel
1 stick plus 2 tsp (4½ oz./125 g) unsalted butter, well chilled and cut into dice
1 egg yolk
3½ tbsp (50 ml) water or milk

Sift the flour and salt into a large bowl, rub in the butter with your fingertips until a sandy texture is obtained, and then stir in the egg yolk. Add the water or milk and work the dough until it comes together into a ball. Flatten into a disk, cover with plastic wrap, and chill in the refrigerator for 20–30 minutes.

VARIATIONS:
1. **Sweet pastry dough with cinnamon**: Add ½ cup (3½ oz./100 g) granulated sugar and 2 tablespoons ground cinnamon with the flour.
2. **Sweet pastry dough with thyme**: Add ½ cup (3½ oz./100 g) granulated cane sugar and the leaves of 5 fresh thyme sprigs with the flour.
3. **Savory pastry dough**: Add finely chopped fresh rosemary, oregano, or thyme leaves (or a blend of fresh herbs) with the flour. You could even add tiny bits of smoked bacon.

KITCHEN NOTES: When making a fruit tart on a warm summer day, I prepare it with the filling and chill it in the refrigerator for about 15 minutes before baking. This prevents the butter in the dough from melting right away when the tart goes in the oven.

CUMIN
AND LEMON SALT

Makes just over ½ cup

ACTIVE TIME
15 minutes

INGREDIENTS
2 tsp cumin seeds
2 tsp finely grated lemon zest
½ cup Himalayan salt or fleur de sel

1. Toast the cumin seeds in a dry skillet over low heat.
2. Place the seeds in a mortar with the lemon zest and salt and pound together with a pestle until well blended. This salt keeps well for several months in an airtight jar.

KITCHEN NOTES: Sprinkle this flavorful finishing salt over your favorite fish dishes, soups, or salads.

HOMEMADE ZA'ATAR

Makes about ¾ cup

ACTIVE TIME
10 minutes

INGREDIENTS
2 tbsp toasted sesame seeds
2 tbsp dried oregano
2 tbsp cumin seeds
2 tbsp dried savory
2 tbsp dried thyme
1 tbsp dried lemon zest
2 tsp sumac
Salt and freshly ground pepper
Extra-virgin olive oil (optional,
    for making a spread)

1. Place all of the ingredients, except for the olive oil, in a mortar and pound with a pestle until well blended. Store in an airtight jar and use within several weeks.
2. To make a za'atar spread for toast, tarts, or vegetables, add a drizzle of olive oil to the dry mix and pound to a paste in the mortar. This spread is best when used right away, but leftovers can be refrigerated in an airtight container and used within a week.

FRESH HERB-INFUSED OLIVE OIL

Makes ½ cup (120 ml)

ACTIVE TIME
10 minutes

INFUSING TIME
1 week

INGREDIENTS
3 small sprigs fresh thyme
2 sprigs fresh rosemary
½ cup (120 ml) extra-virgin olive oil

1. Rinse the herbs under warm water and gently dry with paper towel or a dish towel, making sure no trace of moisture remains.
2. Finely chop the herbs (or leave them whole) and place in a jar. Cover with the olive oil and tightly close the jar with a lid. Let infuse for 1 week in the refrigerator. If you wish, strain the oil through a fine-mesh sieve before using. Refrigerate any unused oil and consume within 1 week at the most.

KITCHEN NOTES: Try swapping the rosemary and thyme for other seasonings like peppercorns, lemon peel, chili peppers, cilantro, or basil.

CARROT-TOP PESTO

Makes about 1½ cups

ACTIVE TIME
15 minutes

INGREDIENTS
Tops from 1 bunch carrots
½ cup (2 oz./60 g) toasted cashews
Generous ½ cup (2 oz./60 g) grated Parmesan
Extra-virgin olive oil
Salt and freshly ground pepper

1. Rinse and roughly chop the carrot tops. Place in a food processor.
2. Add the cashews, Parmesan, and salt and pepper to taste. Process until well blended.
3. With the food processor running, gradually drizzle in olive oil until the pesto reaches the desired consistency. Taste and add more salt and pepper if necessary. Store in an airtight container in the refrigerator for up to 1 week.

KITCHEN NOTES: This pesto not only makes a delicious pasta sauce, but it is also excellent in vinaigrettes or on crostini, for instance.

APRICOT CHUTNEY

Makes about 3 cups

ACTIVE TIME
10 minutes

COOKING TIME
1 hour 5 minutes

INGREDIENTS
3 cooking apples of your choice
5 fresh apricots
10 dried apricots
1 large yellow onion, thinly sliced
1 tsp kosher salt
2 tbsp golden raisins
2 tbsp dried blueberries
¼ cup (60 ml) distilled white vinegar
2⅓ cups (1 lb./450 g) granulated sugar

1. Peel, core, and cut the apples into small pieces. Remove the pits from the fresh apricots and cut into small pieces. Chop the dried apricots into small pieces.
2. Combine all of the ingredients, except for the sugar, in a large saucepan. Bring to a boil, then reduce the heat and simmer for 45 minutes, to allow the mixture to reduce and thicken. Remove from the heat and stir in the sugar.
3. Return the pan to low heat and simmer for an additional 20 minutes, stirring occasionally. Let cool for several minutes before transferring to sterilized jars. Seal tightly and store in a cool, dark place. Once opened, keep it in the refrigerator and use within a week.

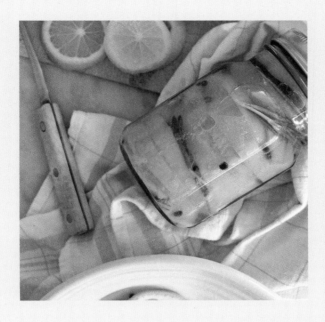

PRESERVED LEMONS

Makes about 2 cups

ACTIVE TIME
15 minutes

RESTING TIME
1 week

INGREDIENTS
3 lemons, preferably organic
3 Meyer lemons, preferably organic
2 tbsp black peppercorns
4 sprigs fresh rosemary
4 tbsp kosher salt, divided

1. Trim off the ends of the lemons. Cut each lemon into ½-inch (1-cm) slices.
2. In a large bowl, gently combine the lemon slices, peppercorns, rosemary sprigs, and 2 tablespoons kosher salt.
3. Place 1 tablespoon kosher salt in the base of a 2-cup (470-ml) jar and arrange the lemon slices, peppercorns, and rosemary sprigs on top. Gently press down on the lemons with your fingertips to release some of the juices and cover with the remaining salt. Close the jar tightly.
4. Let rest for 20 minutes, then turn the jar upside down and store in this position at room temperature for at least 1 week, preferably 2, before using. Once opened, store in the refrigerator and use within 3 months.

COCKTAIL HOUR

WARM HERB-SEASONED NUTS

Serves 6–8

ACTIVE TIME
5 minutes

COOKING TIME
10 minutes

INGREDIENTS
2¼ lb. (1 kg) assorted raw unsalted nuts
    (hazelnuts, cashews, almonds, Brazil nuts,
    pecans, etc.)
Extra-virgin olive oil
Fresh herbs of your choice (thyme, rosemary,
    oregano, etc.), finely chopped
1 pinch cayenne pepper (optional)
Fleur de sel
Freshly ground pepper

1. Preheat the oven to 350°F (180°C/Gas Mark 4) and line a rimmed baking sheet with parchment paper.
2. Spread the nuts across the baking sheet, drizzle with olive oil, and sprinkle with fleur de sel. Toss to coat.
3. Bake for 10 minutes, until toasted and fragrant, stirring halfway through.
4. Remove the nuts from the baking sheet and while they are still warm, stir in the herbs and season with pepper. Sprinkle in the cayenne pepper if you want to add a little spice. Serve warm.

ROSEMARY-RHUBARB COOLER

Makes 4 cocktails

ACTIVE TIME
5 minutes

COOKING TIME
5 minutes

INFUSING TIME
15 minutes

INGREDIENTS
1 lb. 5 oz. (600 g) young, pink-stemmed rhubarb, divided
1½ cups (10½ oz./300 g) superfine sugar
¾ cup (200 ml) water
4 sprigs fresh rosemary with flowers, divided
2 lemons, preferably organic
¾ cup (200 ml) vodka
Large ice cubes
About 2 cups (500 ml) sparkling water

1. Wash the rhubarb and cut 1 lb. 2 oz. (500 g) into small pieces, and the remaining 3 oz. (100 g) into 4 large pieces for garnish. Place the small rhubarb pieces in a large saucepan with the sugar, water, and 3 rosemary sprigs. Heat until the sugar dissolves, then boil for 5 minutes to make a syrup. Remove from the heat and let infuse for 15 minutes.
2. Strain the syrup through a fine-mesh sieve and place 2 tablespoons of syrup in each of 4 glasses.
3. Top the syrup in each glass with the juice of ½ lemon and 3½ tbsp (50 ml) vodka. Add 4–5 ice cubes and a splash of sparkling water per drink. Stir to combine.
4. Garnish with pieces of the remaining rosemary sprig and rhubarb before serving.

AVOCADO TOAST WITH THYME AND WHITE TRUFFLE OIL

Serves 4

ACTIVE TIME
10 minutes

INGREDIENTS
4 large slices country bread
2 avocados, sliced
White truffle oil
A few sprigs fresh thyme with flowers
Fleur de sel
Freshly ground pepper

1. Toast the bread and cut the slices in half crosswise.
2. Arrange the avocado slices on the toast pieces and season with fleur de sel and pepper. Sprinkle with a few drops of white truffle oil.
3. Garnish with the thyme sprigs and serve.

SUMMER LEMON COCKTAIL WITH FRESH THYME SYRUP

Makes 4 cocktails

ACTIVE TIME
5 minutes

COOKING TIME
7 minutes

INFUSING TIME
15 minutes

INGREDIENTS
1 cup (7 oz./200 g) superfine sugar
Scant 1 cup (235 ml) water
½ bunch fresh thyme, divided
1⅔ cups (400 ml) gin
5 lemons, preferably organic
12–16 large ice cubes
Sparkling water
4 lemon slices, preferably organic, for garnish

1. In a small saucepan, combine the sugar and water. Add the thyme, reserving 4 sprigs for garnish. Heat until the sugar dissolves, bring to a boil, lower the heat, and simmer for 5 minutes.
2. Remove from the heat and let infuse for 15 minutes. Remove the thyme sprigs.
3. Place 3 tablespoons of syrup in the base of each of 4 glasses. Add a scant ½ cup (100 ml) gin and the juice of 1 lemon per cocktail. Stir.
4. Divide the ice cubes among the glasses and top off with sparkling water. Garnish each drink with a thyme sprig and lemon slice. Serve cold.

See photo pp. 40–41

APRICOT AND
FIG CROSTINI

Serves 4

ACTIVE TIME
10 minutes

INGREDIENTS
4 large slices country bread
Extra-virgin olive oil
5¼ oz. (150 g) fresh goat cheese
Zest of 1 lemon, preferably organic, finely grated
3 apricots
3 figs
12 baby spinach leaves
Honey
Fleur de sel
Freshly ground pepper

1. Toast the bread and cut each slice into three pieces. Drizzle with olive oil.
2. In a bowl, combine the goat cheese and lemon zest until well blended. Season with fleur de sel and pepper, and spread onto the toast pieces.
3. Wash and quarter the apricots and figs.
4. Set 1 apricot slice and 1 fig slice on each crostini, followed by 1 baby spinach leaf and a drizzle of honey. Sprinkle with fleur de sel and pepper, and serve.

See photo p. 40–41

SEA BREAM TARTARE WITH MANGO AND CILANTRO

Serves 5

ACTIVE TIME
10 minutes

INGREDIENTS
1 lb. (500 g) skinless, boneless sea bream fillets
1 mango
½ bunch cilantro
1 red onion
Juice of 1 lime, preferably organic
4 tbsp extra-virgin olive oil
1 tsp coriander seeds, crushed
10 outer leaves of Little Gem lettuce,
    washed and dried
Salt and freshly ground pepper

1. Finely dice the sea bream. Peel and dice the mango flesh, finely chop the cilantro, and mince the red onion.
2. In a bowl, combine the sea bream, mango, cilantro, red onion, lime juice, olive oil, and coriander seeds. Season with a pinch of salt and pepper.
3. Divide the tartare among the Little Gem lettuce leaves and serve well chilled.

ROASTED CAMEMBERT

Serves 4–5

ACTIVE TIME
5 minutes

COOKING TIME
15 minutes

INGREDIENTS
1 wheel Camembert, preferably made with raw
    milk, in a wooden box, at room temperature
1 clove garlic, thinly sliced
A few sprigs fresh rosemary with flowers
Honey
1–1½ oz. (30–40 g) toasted hazelnuts, roughly
    chopped
White truffle oil
Toasted bread, for serving

1. Preheat the oven to 325°F (170°C/Gas Mark 3). Take the Camembert out of its wooden box
   and remove the wrapper. Nestle the base of the box into the top, line with a piece of
   parchment paper, and set the cheese within. Using a knife, score the cheese here and
   there.
2. Tuck a slice of garlic and a piece of rosemary sprig into each incision.
3. Drizzle the cheese with honey and bake for 15 minutes, until the rind is lightly golden.
4. Just before serving, sprinkle the hazelnuts and a few drops of truffle oil over the
   cheese. Serve warm with the toasted bread.

WATERMELON AND VODKA SORBET-FILLED LEMONS

Serves 8

ACTIVE TIME
15 minutes

FREEZING TIME
4 hours

INGREDIENTS
4 lemons, preferably organic
3 slices watermelon, rind removed
Scant ½ cup (100 ml) vodka
Leaves of 3 sprigs fresh lemon verbena,
　divided
10 large ice cubes

1. Cut the lemons in half lengthwise and gently scoop out the pulp with a spoon. Set the lemon shells aside.
2. Place the pulp of 3 lemon halves in a countertop blender (you can make lemonade with the rest). Add the watermelon, vodka, two-thirds of the lemon verbena leaves, and the ice cubes. Blend until smooth.
3. Pour the mixture into the lemon shells, filling them three-quarters full.
4. Place in the freezer for at least 4 hours. Before serving, garnish with the remaining lemon verbena leaves.

BELLINI-STYLE GRANITA

Makes 6–8 cocktails

ACTIVE TIME
10 minutes

FREEZING TIME
5 hours

INGREDIENTS
10 white Saturn peaches
Juice of ½ lemon, preferably organic
¾ cup (5 oz./150 g) superfine sugar
1½ cups (350 ml) champagne or prosecco
A few small sprigs fresh thyme with flowers,
    for garnish

1. Peel and chop the peaches and place in a blender with the lemon juice and sugar.
   Process until smooth.
2. Blend in the champagne or prosecco, then transfer the mixture to a freezer container
   (I like to use a Pyrex glass dish). Cover and freeze for at least 5 hours.
3. To serve, scrape the frozen granita with a fork to produce melt-in-your-mouth flakes.
   Divide among 6 to 8 glasses and garnish with the thyme sprigs. Serve immediately.

PEACH AND PROSCIUTTO PIZZA

Serves 6–8

ACTIVE TIME
10 minutes

COOKING TIME
25 minutes

INGREDIENTS
About 12 oz. (350 g) pizza dough
¾ lb. (350 g) fresh goat cheese
Leaves of 3–4 sprigs fresh lemon thyme
3 yellow peaches
Extra-virgin olive oil
1 large handful fresh arugula
6 slices prosciutto, cut into pieces
Salt and freshly ground pepper

1. Preheat the oven to 375°F (190°C/Gas Mark 5). Stretch or roll out the pizza dough into a thin oval and set it on a baking sheet lined with parchment paper.
2. In a large bowl, combine the goat cheese, lemon thyme, and salt and pepper to taste. Spread evenly over the pizza dough, leaving a narrow border around the edges.
3. Rinse and quarter the peaches with the skin on.
4. Arrange the peach quarters over the goat cheese mixture and drizzle with olive oil. Bake for 20–25 minutes, until the crust and peaches are lightly golden.
5. Top the warm pizza with the arugula and prosciutto, add a few grinds of fresh pepper, and serve immediately.

KITCHEN NOTES: This pizza is equally delicious with fresh figs or apricots instead of peaches.

END OF SUMMER COCKTAIL

Makes 6 cocktails

ACTIVE TIME
10 minutes

INFUSING TIME
15 minutes

INGREDIENTS
⅔ cup (150 ml) water
Scant ¾ cup (5¼ oz./150 g) demerara sugar
6 long sprigs fresh rosemary, divided
12 plums, such as greengage or Golden Japan
Juice of ½ lemon, preferably organic
Several large ice cubes
1 bottle prosecco, well chilled
2 Black Amber plums, thinly sliced, for garnish

1. Heat the water in a saucepan, add the sugar, and stir until the sugar has fully dissolved.
2. Add 4 rosemary sprigs to the syrup, stir, and remove from the heat. Let infuse for 15 minutes, then remove the rosemary.
3. Wash, pit, and cut the 12 plums into pieces. Place in a blender with the lemon juice and process until smooth. Strain through a fine-mesh sieve.
4. Put 1 tablespoon of rosemary syrup in the base of 6 tumblers or whisky glasses, followed by 1 tablespoon of plum puree. Stir.
5. Place a few large ice cubes in each glass and fill with prosecco. Stir to combine and garnish with the remaining rosemary sprigs and Black Amber plum slices. Serve immediately.

GOAT CHEESE, CRANBERRY, AND PECAN BITES

Makes about 30

ACTIVE TIME
10 minutes

SOAKING TIME
5–7 minutes

COOKING TIME
20 minutes

INGREDIENTS
1 large handful dried cranberries
2 sheets puff pastry, preferably all butter
5¼ oz. (150 g) fresh goat cheese
Scant ½ cup (1¾ oz./50 g) pecans, finely
  chopped
Honey
A few sprigs fresh rosemary or thyme,
  for garnish

1. Preheat the oven to 350°F (180°C/Gas Mark 4). Meanwhile, soak the cranberries in a bowl of warm water for 5–7 minutes to allow them to soften and swell slightly. Drain well.
2. Spread out the puff pastry sheets and cut them into 2 × 2¾-inch (5 × 7-cm) squares.
3. Press the squares into the cavities of mini muffin pans and fill each with a dollop of goat cheese, 2 or 3 cranberries, a sprinkling of pecans, and a few drops of honey.
4. Bake for 15–20 minutes, until the pastry is puffed and golden.
5. Garnish with the rosemary or thyme sprigs and serve.

FESTIVE CIDER

Makes 8 cocktails

ACTIVE TIME
10 minutes

INGREDIENTS
1 tbsp plus 2 tsp (⅔ oz./20 g) superfine sugar
8 pinches ground cinnamon, divided
1 bottle hard apple cider, preferably naturally
    fermented, well chilled
1 bottle champagne or prosecco,
    well chilled
Several large ice cubes
8 cinnamon sticks, for garnish

1. In a small, shallow bowl, combine the sugar with 6 pinches of cinnamon.
2. Wet the rim of each of 8 glasses and dip into the cinnamon sugar.
3. Carefully fill the glasses halfway with cider and top off with champagne
   or prosecco.
4. Add a few large ice cubes to each drink and sprinkle with the remaining cinnamon.
   Garnish with the cinnamon sticks and serve immediately.

CHEESE SHORTBREADS

Makes about 30

ACTIVE TIME
10 minutes

CHILLING TIME
1 hour

COOKING TIME
15 minutes

INGREDIENTS
1 stick plus 1 tsp (4¼ oz./120 g) unsalted butter,
  well chilled and diced
1¾ cups (7 oz./200 g) shredded mature Cheddar
½ cup (1¾ oz./50 g) grated Parmesan
½ tsp cayenne pepper
1 cup (4½ oz./130 g) all-purpose flour
12 pecan halves
2 sprigs fresh rosemary
3 sprigs fresh thyme
Kosher salt
Freshly ground black pepper

1. In a large bowl, combine the butter, cheeses, cayenne pepper, flour, and a pinch of kosher salt using your fingertips. When the dough comes together, shape it into a large ball.
2. Divide the dough in two and shape each half into a log with a diameter of 2½–2¾ inches (6–7 cm). Cover with plastic wrap and chill in the refrigerator for at least 1 hour.
3. Preheat the oven to 350°F (180°C/Gas Mark 4) and line a baking sheet with parchment paper. Cut the chilled dough logs into ¼-inch (0.5-cm) slices and place on the baking sheet.
4. Top each slice with either a pecan half or a small sprig of rosemary or thyme, lightly pressing them into the dough, and bake for 15 minutes. While the shortbreads are still warm, sprinkle them with kosher salt and pepper. Let cool and serve.

STARTERS

ASPARAGUS AND PEA TART

Serves 6–8

ACTIVE TIME
15 minutes

COOKING TIME
30 minutes

CHILLING TIME
10 minutes

INGREDIENTS
¾ cup (200 ml) oat-based cream alternative
1 handful unsalted cashews
3 tbsp (3 oz./80 g) mint pesto (see Kitchen
　Notes)
2 bunches thin green asparagus
Generous ½ cup (3 oz./80 g) fresh green peas
12 sheets phyllo dough
Zest of 1 lemon, preferably organic
Shaved Parmesan
A few tiny sprigs dill
Dukkah spice mix (optional)
Kosher salt and freshly ground pepper

1. Preheat the oven to 350°F (180°C/Gas Mark 4).
2. Place the oat cream, cashews, and pesto in a food processor or blender and process until smooth. Season with salt and pepper and chill in the refrigerator for about 10 minutes.
3. Rinse and gently dry the asparagus and peas. Cut the tough bottom ends off the asparagus spears, leaving the stalks long.
4. Line a baking sheet with parchment paper and brush the paper with a thin layer of olive oil. Set the first layer of phyllo dough flat on the baking sheet, brush lightly with olive oil, and top with another phyllo sheet. Repeat with the remaining phyllo dough. If you like, sprinkle a bit of kosher salt and pepper between some of the layers.
5. Spread the oat cream mixture over the top layer of phyllo dough, leaving a 1¼ –1½-inch (3–4-cm) border. Line up the asparagus spears side by side over the cream mixture, alternating directions. Scatter the peas over the top.
6. Bake for 25–30 minutes, until the pastry is golden and the asparagus al dente.
7. Let the tart cool for 10 minutes, then sprinkle with the lemon zest, Parmesan, dill sprigs, and a little dukkah if using.

KITCHEN NOTES: To make mint pesto, simply use mint instead of basil in your normal pesto recipe, or swap out the pine nuts for hazelnuts, cashews, etc. Cut into bite-sized pieces, this tart makes a great cocktail hour snack.

GREEN BEAN SALAD WITH HAZELNUTS AND PARMESAN

Serves 4

ACTIVE TIME
10 minutes

COOKING TIME
5 minutes

INGREDIENTS
2 lb. (1 kg) green beans
2 tsp whole grain mustard
2 tbsp balsamic vinegar
2 tbsp extra-virgin olive oil
2 tbsp hazelnut oil
1 shallot, thinly sliced
2 tbsp crushed toasted hazelnuts
2 handfuls arugula
1 handful shaved Parmesan
1 handful dried cranberries or blueberries
A few arugula or amaranth sprouts (optional)
Salt and freshly ground pepper

1. Blanch the green beans in generously salted water for 5 minutes.
2. Plunge the beans into a large bowl filled with ice water. After 1 minute, drain and dry the beans.
3. In the base of a large salad bowl, prepare the vinaigrette: Combine the mustard, vinegar, extra-virgin olive oi, and hazelnut oil, then season with salt and pepper.
4. Add the green beans, hazelnuts, shallot, and dried cranberries or blueberries to the salad bowl and toss with the vinaigrette.
5. Before serving, sprinkle the salad with the arugula, Parmesan, and amaranth sprouts if using.

KITCHEN NOTES: For a non-vegetarian version of this salad, you could toss in bits of smoked bacon, fried until crisp.

SWEET AND SAVORY RHUBARB TORTILLAS

Serves 4

ACTIVE TIME
15 minutes

COOKING TIME
10 minutes

INGREDIENTS
2 stalks rhubarb
1 tbsp maple syrup
Extra-virgin olive oil
4 tortillas of your choice
1 cup (9 oz./250 g) ricotta
4 green scallion tops, thinly sliced
Zest of 1 organic lemon
3½ oz. (100 g) arugula
1 medium yellow carrot, peeled and grated
Pickled red onions
2 dates
⅓ cup (1¾ oz./50 g) toasted hazelnuts, crushed
Leaves of 3 sprigs fresh mint, chopped
Salt and freshly ground pepper

1. Preheat the oven to 400°F (200°C/Gas Mark 6).
2. Cut the rhubarb stalks into ½–¾-inch (1–2-cm) pieces and place on a baking sheet. Drizzle with the maple syrup and stir to coat.
3. Bake for 7–8 minutes, until the rhubarb is tender and lightly caramelized around the edges.
4. Lightly brown the tortillas on both sides in a hot skillet with a small amount of oil.
5. In a bowl, whisk together the ricotta, half the scallion tops, and half the lemon zest until well blended. Season with salt and pepper.
6. Spread each tortilla with the ricotta mixture and top with a small mound of arugula. Sprinkle with the grated carrot, followed by the roasted rhubarb and several slices of pickled red onion.
7. Pit the dates and cut them into 6 slivers lengthwise; divide among the tortillas. Scatter over the remaining scallion tops and lemon zest, followed by the hazelnuts and mint.

WATERCRESS AND ALMOND SOUP

Serves 4–6

ACTIVE TIME
10 minutes

COOKING TIME
30 minutes

INGREDIENTS
2 bunches watercress
2 small potatoes, peeled and diced
2 cups (500 ml) water
1 bouillon cube (vegetable or chicken)
1 yellow onion, finely chopped
Extra-virgin olive oil
1 handful blanched almonds
1 handful toasted pumpkin seeds
Heavy cream
Kosher salt
Freshly ground pepper

1. Wash the watercress and set aside a few attractive leaves for garnish; roughly chop the rest. Place in a large saucepan with the potatoes, water, bouillon cube, and a pinch of kosher salt. Cook over medium heat for 20–25 minutes, until the potatoes are tender.
2. Meanwhile, sauté the onion in a skillet with a small amount of olive oil and a pinch of salt until very soft.
3. Place the potatoes and watercress in a blender along with 1 or 2 ladlefuls of broth, depending on how thick you want the soup. Process until smooth. Season with salt and pepper to taste.
4. Toast the almonds in a dry skillet over medium heat, stirring frequently to prevent burning. If you wish, chop the almonds roughly.
5. To serve, pour the soup into bowls or soup plates and sprinkle with the watercress leaves, almonds, and pumpkin seeds. Add a swirl of cream and a few grinds of pepper and serve.

WHITE TRUFFLE-FLAVORED ZUCCHINI TART

Serves 6

ACTIVE TIME
20 minutes

COOKING TIME
20 minutes

INGREDIENTS
1 sheet puff pastry (rectangle or square),
   preferably all butter
3 tbsp (3 oz./80 g) basil pesto
3-4 zucchini and/or yellow squash
1 egg yolk, beaten
1 handful pine nuts
1 ball burrata cheese (about 8 oz./250 g)
1 handful arugula
A few leaves of fresh basil
Finely grated zest of 1 organic lemon,
3½ oz. (100 g) shaved Parmesan
1 white truffle or a drizzle of white truffle oil
Kosher salt
Freshly ground pepper

1. Preheat the oven to 350°F (180°C/Gas Mark 4) and line a baking sheet with parchment paper.
2. Place the puff pastry on the baking sheet and spread with a thin layer of pesto, leaving a narrow border around the edges.
3. Using a vegetable peeler, make long, thin ribbons of zucchini and/or yellow squash and arrange over the pesto.
4. Brush the edges of the pastry with the egg yolk and sprinkle the tart with kosher salt and pepper.
5. Bake for 20 minutes, until the crust is golden.
6. Meanwhile, place a dry skillet over medium heat, add the pine nuts, and toast lightly. Remove from the pan.
7. Remove the tart from the oven, cut the burrata into pieces, and scatter over the top.
8. Distribute the pine nuts, arugula, basil leaves, lemon zest, and Parmesan evenly over the tart.
9. Finish with a few shavings of white truffle or a drizzle of white truffle oil and serve.

STUFFED ARTICHOKES

Serves 5

ACTIVE TIME
10 minutes

COOKING TIME
40 minutes

INGREDIENTS
5 globe artichokes
3 lemons, preferably organic
2 cloves garlic, finely chopped
Extra-virgin olive oil
3 cups (10½ oz./300 g) bread crumbs
Leaves of 3 sprigs fresh parsley, chopped
Leaves of 3 sprigs fresh basil, chopped
1½ cups (5¼ oz./50 g) Parmesan, grated
Salt and freshly ground pepper

1. Cut off the base and the top 1¼ inches (3 cm) of each artichoke and remove the tough outer layer of leaves.
2. Grate the zest and squeeze the juice from 2 of the lemons. Set the zest aside and pour the juice over the artichokes to prevent browning.
3. Steam the artichokes for 20 minutes and let cool.
4. Meanwhile, juice the remaining lemon, then sauté the garlic in a skillet over medium heat with a small amount of olive oil and a pinch of salt. When the garlic begins to color, stir in the lemon juice, bread crumbs, parsley, and basil.
5. Season to taste with salt and pepper, stir in the lemon zest, and remove from the heat.
6. Preheat the oven to 350°F (180°C/Gas Mark 4). Remove the inner leaves from the center of each artichoke and scoop out the chokes with a teaspoon.
7. Stir the Parmesan into the bread crumb mixture, then stuff this filling into the cavity of each artichoke, packing some between the leaves as well. Sit the artichokes close together in a single layer in a baking dish, drizzle with olive oil, and bake for 15–20 minutes, until the artichokes are completely tender and the bread crumbs golden. Serve hot or warm.

PEA AND
ASPARAGUS SOUP

Serves 4

ACTIVE TIME
10 minutes

COOKING TIME
15 minutes

INGREDIENTS
1 yellow onion, thinly sliced
1 leek, white part only, thinly sliced and rinsed
1 vegetable bouillon cube
1¾ cups (9 oz./250 g) green peas
2 bunches thin green asparagus
Scant ⅔ cup (5¼ oz./150 g) ricotta
1 piece preserved lemon (see recipe p. 31),
    thinly sliced
2 tbsp toasted almonds, finely chopped
Extra-virgin olive oil
Salt and freshly ground pepper

1. In a skillet over low heat, cook the onion and leek in a small amount of olive oil until soft.
2. Trim off the bottom ends of the asparagus and cut all but 6 of the stalks into 2 pieces. Fill a large saucepan with water and bring to a boil; crumble in the bouillon cube and stir until dissolved. Add the asparagus and peas, reduce the heat to a simmer, and cook for 10 minutes.
3. Set aside the whole asparagus stalks for garnish and place the remaining stalks in a blender with the peas and broth (start with less broth if you want a thicker soup). Add the onion and leek and process until smooth.
4. Blend in the ricotta and season with salt and pepper.
5. Just before serving, garnish the soup with the preserved lemon slices and toasted almonds. Cut the reserved asparagus stalks in half lengthwise and add as a final flourish. Serve hot or cold.

SARDINE, ARUGULA, AND PARMESAN SALAD

Serves 4

ACTIVE TIME
5 minutes

COOKING TIME
5 minutes

INGREDIENTS
5 oz. (150 g) arugula
8 canned sardines in olive oil
Fresh herbs (dill, basil, tarragon, etc.), roughly
   chopped
12 Kalamata olives
Generous ½ cup (2 oz./60 g) shaved Parmesan
Several slices preserved lemon
   (see recipe p. 31)
2 tbsp jarred capers, drained
Salt and freshly ground pepper

1. Scatter the arugula across the base of a serving dish.
2. Arrange the sardines over the arugula and sprinkle with the fresh herbs, olives, and Parmesan. Cut the preserved lemons into slivers and scatter over the salad.
3. In a skillet, fry the capers for 5 minutes over high heat until crisp and golden. Sprinkle over the salad. Season with salt and pepper and serve with country bread.

ASPARAGUS AND HAZELNUT SALAD

Serves 5

ACTIVE TIME
10 minutes

COOKING TIME
5 minutes

INGREDIENTS
2 bunches thin green asparagus
Finely grated zest of 1 lemon, preferably
  organic
2 scallions, green parts only, thinly sliced
A few pickled red onion slices
1 handful toasted hazelnuts, roughly chopped
Leaves of 3 sprigs fresh parsley, roughly
  chopped
3 tbsp extra-virgin olive oil
Salt and freshly ground pepper

1. Wash the asparagus and trim off the bottom ends. Bring a large saucepan of generously salted water to a boil, add the asparagus, and blanch for 5 minutes. Transfer to a large bowl filled with ice water to stop the cooking.
2. Drain the asparagus and wrap it in a dish towel to dry. Arrange on a serving platter.
3. Add the lemon zest to the asparagus and gently combine.
4. Sprinkle the scallions and pickled red onions over the asparagus.
5. Top with the hazelnuts and parsley.
6. In a small bowl, combine the olive oil, lemon juice, and salt and pepper to taste. Drizzle over the salad and serve.

STEAK TARTARE WITH HAZELNUTS AND PARMESAN

Serves 5

ACTIVE TIME
10 minutes

COOKING TIME
15 minutes

INGREDIENTS
10 slices country bread
Scant ½ cup (2 oz./60 g) hazelnuts,
    with their skins on
1 lb. (500 g) top-quality beef tenderloin
    (see Kitchen Notes)
8 cornichons, thinly sliced
Scant ½ cup (1½ oz./40 g) shaved Parmesan,
    plus more for garnish
Leaves of 2 sprigs fresh basil, chopped
4 tbsp extra-virgin olive oil
Leaves of 1 sprig fresh basil, for garnish
1 drizzle white truffle oil (optional)
Salt and freshly ground pepper

1. Toast the bread until crisp, either in a toaster or under the broiler for 6–7 minutes, turning the slices over halfway through the cooking time.
2. In a dry skillet over medium heat, toast the hazelnuts until golden and fragrant, about 8 minutes, stirring frequently to prevent burning. Let cool slightly, remove the skins, and chop roughly.
3. Chop the beef finely, just before it is needed for maximum freshness.
4. In a large bowl, combine the beef, cornichons, Parmesan, basil, hazelnuts, and olive oil. Season with salt and pepper.
5. Place a small amount of tartare on each slice of toast. Sprinkle with a little shaved Parmesan and the basil leaves. Drizzle with white truffle oil if you wish and serve immediately.

KITCHEN NOTES: To ensure maximum quality and freshness, it is best to purchase your beef from a trusted butcher, and let the butcher know you will be eating the meat raw. It should be in a single piece and must be cut with a knife sterilized in hot water, not chopped in a food processor.

ROASTED TOMATO SOUP

Serves 5–6

ACTIVE TIME
15 minutes

COOKING TIME
1 hour

INGREDIENTS
2¼ lb. (1 kg) assorted tomatoes (cherry, beefsteak, pineapple, etc.)
2 red onions, quartered
4 cloves garlic, unpeeled
3 tbsp extra-virgin olive oil
2 tbsp balsamic vinegar
2 tsp sugar
Leaves of 3 sprigs fresh thyme
Leaves of 3 sprigs fresh basil
1½ cups (350 ml) warm vegetable broth
Salt and freshly ground pepper

1. Preheat the oven to 325°F (160°C/Gas Mark 3).
2. Rinse the tomatoes, cut them in half, and set on a rimmed baking sheet with the cut side up.
3. Place the onions on the baking sheet, then crush the garlic cloves with the flat side of a chef's knife and scatter them around the tomatoes and onions.
4. Drizzle with the olive oil and balsamic vinegar, sprinkle with the sugar and thyme leaves, and season with salt and pepper. Roast for 50 minutes, then turn on the broiler and cook for an additional 5–10 minutes, until the tomatoes and onions are lightly charred and caramelized.
5. Remove the skin from the garlic cloves and place in a blender with the tomatoes, onions, any pan juices, and the basil. Process until smooth, adding the warm broth in two or three stages, until the soup reaches your preferred consistency. Serve warm or cold.

TOMATO AND
PEACH SALAD

Serves 6

ACTIVE TIME
10 minutes

INGREDIENTS
6 tbsp balsamic vinegar
6 tbsp extra-virgin olive oil
2 tbsp honey
6 ripe peaches
6 large tomatoes (red and yellow)
15 cherry tomatoes
1 red onion, thinly sliced
Generous ½ cup (2 oz./60 g) pecan halves
Leaves of 1 small bunch basil, roughly
   chopped (reserve a few small leaves
   for garnish)
3½ oz. (100 g) feta, crumbled
Fleur de sel
Freshly ground pepper

1. In a bowl, combine the balsamic vinegar, olive oil, and honey. Season with salt and pepper.
2. Wash and quarter the peaches (with the skin on) and the large tomatoes. Wash the cherry tomatoes and cut them in half crosswise.
3. Place the peaches, tomatoes, and red onion in a large salad bowl and gently stir together.
4. Stir in the pecans, basil, and feta. Just before serving, gently toss in the vinaigrette and garnish with a few basil leaves.

ROASTED EGGPLANT
WITH PRESERVED LEMON,
CAPERS, AND PISTACHIOS

Serves 4

ACTIVE TIME
10 minutes

COOKING TIME
40 minutes

INGREDIENTS
1 large eggplant (or 2 small)
Extra-virgin olive oil
3 pieces preserved lemon (see recipe p. 31),
    finely chopped
2 tbsp pine nuts
2 tbsp jarred capers, drained
1 pinch Cayenne pepper
3 cloves garlic, peeled
1 ball burrata cheese (about 8 oz./250 g), sliced,
    or labneh
2 tbsp roughly chopped pistachios
Leaves of 3 sprigs fresh parsley, roughly
    chopped
Zest of 1 lemon, preferably organic
Salt and freshly ground pepper

1. Preheat the oven to 375°F (190°C/Gas Mark 5).
2. Wash the eggplant and cut it into ½-inch (1-cm) slices with the skin on. Drizzle each slice with a little olive oil and arrange half the slices in a single, slightly overlapping layer in a small baking dish.
3. Scatter half the preserved lemon and half the pine nuts over the first eggplant layer, then top with the remaining eggplant. Sprinkle with the remaining preserved lemon and pine nuts, followed by the capers and Cayenne pepper. Season with salt and pepper.
4. Place the garlic cloves in the dish and bake for 30 minutes, until the eggplant is completely tender. If it is still firm, bake for an additional 10 minutes or longer, as necessary.
5. Right before serving, place the burrata on top of the eggplant in the center of the dish and sprinkle with the pistachios, parsley, and lemon zest.

SUMMER CAULIFLOWER TABBOULEH

Serves 4–5

ACTIVE TIME
10 minutes

COOKING TIME
15 minutes

CHILLING TIME
Overnight

INGREDIENTS
1 large head cauliflower
2 tsp quatre-épices spice mix
4 tbsp extra-virgin olive oil, divided
½ cup (1 ½ oz./40 g) sliced almonds
Seeds of 1 pomegranate
1 small bunch fresh parsley, chopped
3 ½ oz. (100 g) crumbled feta (about ⅔ cup)
Juice of 1 lemon
1 small bunch fresh mint, chopped
Salt and freshly ground pepper

1. Preheat the oven to 375°F (190°C/Gas Mark 5).
2. Remove the outer leaves and tough stalk from the head of cauliflower and cut it into large florets. Place in a food processor and pulse until the cauliflower resembles couscous.
3. Transfer to a large bowl and add the quatre-épices and 2 tablespoons of the olive oil. Season with salt and pepper and toss to combine. Spread the mixture across a rimmed baking sheet in an even layer and bake for 15 minutes, stirring halfway through the cooking. Let cool.
4. Place the cauliflower in a large salad bowl with the almonds, pomegranate seeds, parsley, feta, lemon juice, and the remaining 2 tablespoons olive oil. Toss to combine, then taste and adjust the seasoning as needed.
5. Cover the bowl and refrigerate overnight. When you are ready to serve the salad, give it a stir and sprinkle with the fresh mint.

CAST-IRON SKILLET COCKLES AND CLAMS

Serves 4–6

ACTIVE TIME
10 minutes

COOKING TIME
20 minutes

INGREDIENTS
24 fresh cockles
24 fresh medium-sized clams, such as
    littlenecks, Manila clams or palourdes
2 lemons, preferably organic
Extra-virgin olive oil
1 bunch fresh cilantro, roughly chopped
A few sprigs fresh thyme with their flowers
Fleur de sel
Freshly ground pepper

1. Preheat the oven to 375°F (190°C/Gas Mark 5). Wash the cockles and clams thoroughly in cold water.
2. Quarter the lemons and lightly sear them on all sides in a large cast-iron skillet with 1 tablespoon of olive oil.
3. Remove the skillet from the heat and add the cockles and clams. Drizzle with olive oil, season with fleur de sel and pepper, and stir to combine. Place the skillet in the oven and bake for 15–20 minutes, watching closely and stirring if the cockles and clams are opening unevenly. As soon as all the shells have opened, remove the skillet from the oven. Discard any cockles or clams that remain tightly closed.
4. Sprinkle with the cilantro and thyme, and serve immediately.

WINTER SQUASH SOUP WITH PORCINI CROSTINI

Serves 4–6

ACTIVE TIME
30 minutes

COOKING TIME
50 minutes

INGREDIENTS

1 pumpkin (about 3 lb./1.5 kg)
1 spaghetti squash
   (about 3 lb./1.5 kg)
2 cloves garlic, unpeeled
2 sprigs fresh rosemary
Extra-virgin olive oil
1 leek, sliced
1 yellow onion, sliced
Leaves of 4 sprigs fresh thyme

4 cups (1 L) vegetable or chicken
   broth, warm
4 large porcini mushrooms
1 clove garlic, finely chopped
3 sprigs fresh parsley
4 thick slices country bread
4 tbsp shaved Parmesan
1 drizzle white truffle oil
Toasted pumpkin seeds
   (optional)
Salt and freshly ground pepper

1. Preheat the oven to 425°F (215°C/Gas Mark 7).
2. Wash and halve the pumpkin and spaghetti squash and scoop out the seeds. Cut both into large pieces and set on a baking sheet with the unpeeled garlic cloves and 1 rosemary sprig, and drizzle with olive oil. Season with salt and pepper, stir to coat with the oil, and bake for 30–35 minutes, until the pumpkin and squash are tender.
3. Meanwhile, heat a generous tablespoon of olive oil in a skillet over medium heat, add the leek and onion, and season with salt. Cook for about 10 minutes, stirring occasionally, until softened and browned. Remove from the heat and sprinkle with two-thirds of the thyme leaves.
4. Once the pumpkin and squash are cool enough to handle, scoop the flesh into a food processor or blender, then peel and add the garlic cloves. Add the onion-leek mixture and puree, gradually adding broth until the soup reaches the desired consistency. Taste and adjust the seasoning as needed.
5. To make the crostini, clean the mushrooms with a damp cloth, scrape off any dirt with a knife, and slice thinly. Heat a drizzle of olive oil in a skillet over medium heat and add the mushrooms, parsley, and a pinch of salt. Cook for 7–8 minutes, stirring occasionally, until the mushrooms are tender and browned.
6. Toast the bread and top it with the mushrooms. Finely chop the leaves of the remaining rosemary sprig and sprinkle over the mushrooms, followed by the Parmesan. Drizzle with white truffle oil and season with salt and pepper.
7. Ladle the soup into soup plates and garnish with the remaining thyme leaves and pumpkin seeds if using. Top with the porcini mushroom crostini.

CLAM CHOWDER

Serves 4–6

ACTIVE TIME
20 minutes

COOKING TIME
1 hour

RESTING TIME
1 hour

INGREDIENTS
24 fresh clams, such as littlenecks,
   cherrystones or palourdes
4 cups (1 L) water
1 generous tbsp unsalted butter
5¼ oz. (150 g) smoked slab bacon, diced
2 leeks, white parts only, thinly sliced
1 red onion, thinly sliced
5 small potatoes, peeled and diced
½ cup (115 ml) dry white wine
2 bay leaves
5 sprigs fresh thyme
1⅔ cups (400 ml) heavy cream
Salt and freshly ground pepper

1. Rinse the clams, place them in a Dutch oven with the water, and set over medium heat. Cover and cook until the clams have opened (about 15 minutes). Discard any clams that remain tightly closed.
2. Strain the clam broth through a fine-mesh sieve and set aside. Let the clams cool, remove them from their shells, and set aside.
3. Rinse out the pot, add the butter, and set over low heat. When the butter has melted, stir in the bacon and cook until golden brown (about 5 minutes). Remove the bacon and set aside.
4. Add the sliced leeks and onion to the same pot and stir to coat them in the fat. Cook, stirring frequently, until softened but not browned (about 10 minutes).
5. Add the potatoes and white wine to the pot, stir to combine, and cook until the wine has evaporated. When the potatoes begin to soften, add enough of the clam broth to cover. Add the thyme and bay leaves, partially cover the pot, and cook for about 15 minutes, until the potatoes are completely tender.
6. Meanwhile, cut the clams in half (or into smaller pieces if the clams are large). When the potatoes are ready, stir in the cream, clams, and bacon and season with salt and pepper. Bring to a simmer (not a boil), cook for 5 minutes, and remove from the heat.
7. Let the chowder rest for 1 hour to allow the flavors to develop, then gently reheat and serve.

MINI CHICKEN, MUSHROOM, AND VEGETABLE PIES

Serves 6

ACTIVE TIME
20 minutes

COOKING TIME
35 minutes

INGREDIENTS
1 generous tbsp unsalted butter, for greasing
   the ramekins
3 tbsp extra-virgin olive oil, divided
½ lb. (240 g) chicken breast, diced
6 small white onions, halved
2 carrots, finely diced
8¾ oz. (250 g) cremini mushrooms, wiped clean
   and thinly sliced
3 large cloves garlic, finely chopped
Leaves of 2 sprigs fresh rosemary, chopped
3 tbsp all-purpose flour
2 cups (500 ml) chicken broth
4 tbsp crème fraîche
2 sheets puff pastry
1 egg white, lightly beaten
Generous ⅓ cup (1½ oz./40 g) grated Gruyère
Salt and freshly ground pepper

1. Preheat the oven to 400°F (200°C/Gas Mark 6) and lightly grease 6 ramekins.
2. Heat 2 tablespoons of the olive oil in a large skillet over medium-high heat. Add the chicken breast, season with salt and pepper, and cook until lightly browned. Set the chicken aside on a plate.
3. Add the remaining olive oil to the same skillet and lower the heat to medium. Add the onions and cook, stirring frequently, until softened.
4. Add the carrots and cook until caramelized around the edges, about 5 minutes.
5. Add the mushrooms, garlic, rosemary, and salt and pepper to taste. Cook for an additional 5-6 minutes, until the mushrooms are tender. Set aside several mushroom slices for decoration.
6. Stir in the flour, then gradually pour in the broth, stirring constantly. Incorporate the crème fraîche, then add the chicken and simmer for 5 minutes to thicken the sauce. Remove from the heat.
7. Using a glass or small bowl slightly larger than the ramekins, cut out 12 circles from the puff pastry sheets. Line each ramekin with a pastry circle and fill with the chicken-mushroom mixture. Cover with another pastry circle and pinch the edges of the two circles together to seal. Lightly brush the pastry with the egg white, sprinkle with the Gruyère, and top with a few mushroom slices. Bake for 20 minutes, until puffed and golden.
8. Let the pies cool in the ramekins for about 10 minutes, then carefully turn them out and serve.

MUSHROOM AND PARMESAN SOUP

Serves 5

ACTIVE TIME
25 minutes

COOKING TIME
30 minutes

INGREDIENTS
2¼ lb. (1 kg) assorted mushrooms, such as
  shiitakes and button mushrooms
Juice of 1 lemon
7 tbsp (3½ oz./100 g) unsalted butter

1 clove garlic, finely chopped
2 tbsp all-purpose flour
4 cups (1 L) water
2 bouillon cubes (vegetable or chicken)
2 cups (500 ml) milk
1½ cups (5¼ oz./150 g) grated Parmesan
2 tbsp crème fraîche
2 tbsp extra-virgin olive oil
⅓ cup (1 oz./30 g) shaved Parmesan
Leaves of 2–3 sprigs fresh parsley, finely
  chopped
Salt and freshly ground pepper

1. Clean the mushrooms and trim the ends off the stems. Slice the mushrooms thinly and sprinkle them with the lemon juice.
2. In a saucepan, melt the butter over low heat and add the garlic and mushrooms, reserving a few slices for garnish. Cook, stirring gently, for 5 minutes, then stir in the flour. Add the water and bouillon cubes and bring to a boil. Lower the heat to medium and cook for 15 minutes to reduce.
3. Season with a little salt and pepper, reduce the heat to low, and stir in the milk and grated Parmesan.
4. Transfer to a blender and puree until smooth. Blend in the crème fraîche.
5. In a hot skillet with a little olive oil, brown the reserved mushroom slices.
6. Pour the soup into a tureen and top with the mushroom slices. Sprinkle with the shaved Parmesan, parsley, and a few grinds of pepper, and serve right away.

APPLE, BRIE, AND CARAMELIZED ONION TURNOVERS

Serves 6

ACTIVE TIME
10 minutes

COOKING TIME
20 minutes

INGREDIENTS
1 yellow onion, thinly sliced
1 tbsp extra-virgin olive oil
1 tbsp honey
1 cooking apple, such as Belle de Boskoop,
  Elstar, or Pink Lady
4¼ oz. (120 g) Brie
1 rectangular sheet puff pastry, preferably
  all butter
6 pinches fennel seeds
3 sprigs fresh thyme
1 egg yolk, lightly beaten
Kosher salt
Freshly ground pepper

1. Preheat the oven to 375°F (190°C/Gas Mark 5) and line a baking sheet with parchment paper.
2. Cook the onion in a skillet over low heat with the olive oil and a pinch of salt until translucent. Stir in the honey, increase the heat to medium, and let caramelize for 3–4 minutes. Remove from the heat.
3. Peel, core, and thinly slice the apple.
4. Cut the Brie into 6 equal pieces.
5. Cut the puff pastry into 6 equal rectangles and set on the prepared baking sheet.
6. Place a small mound of caramelized onion in the center of the left-hand side of each rectangle. Divide the apple slices over the onions, followed by the Brie. Top the filling in each pastry rectangle with a pinch of fennel seeds and the leaves from a half-sprig of thyme (use the stems, too, if they are tender). Set aside a few thyme leaves for sprinkling over the turnovers.
7. To close the turnovers, fold the right-hand side of each rectangle over the filling on the left. Press around the edges with the tines of a fork to seal well.
8. Brush the pastry with the egg yolk and sprinkle with the remaining thyme leaves, kosher salt, and pepper.
9. Bake for 15 minutes, until golden brown. Let rest for 5 minutes before serving.

CREAMY ROASTED CAULIFLOWER SOUP

Serves 4–6

ACTIVE TIME
10 minutes

COOKING TIME
35 minutes

INGREDIENTS
1 large head cauliflower
3 cloves garlic, peeled
3 cups (750 ml) water
2 bouillon cubes (vegetable or chicken)
4 tbsp crème fraîche
Scant ⅔ cup (2 oz./60 g) grated Parmesan
Leaves of 4 sprigs fresh thyme
Extra-virgin olive oil
White truffle oil (optional)
Fleur de sel
Kosher salt
Freshly ground pepper

1. Preheat the oven to 350°F (180°C/Gas Mark 4).
2. Remove the outer leaves from the head of cauliflower and wash it. Thinly slice a few florets for garnish, then cut the rest into pieces, removing the tough stalk, and place on a rimmed baking sheet with the garlic cloves. Drizzle with olive oil, sprinkle with fleur de sel, and toss to coat. Roast for 30 minutes, until the cauliflower is tender and caramelized around the edges.
3. In a saucepan, bring the water to a boil and stir in the bouillon cubes to dissolve.
4. Place the roasted cauliflower and garlic in a blender with the crème fraîche, Parmesan, and two-thirds of the thyme. Puree, gradually adding broth until the soup reaches the desired consistency. Taste for salt and pepper.
5. Heat a small amount of olive oil in a skillet over high heat. Add the sliced cauliflower florets you set aside in step 2 and brown them for a few minutes on each side. Season with salt and pepper.
6. Pour the soup into a tureen and arrange the cauliflower slices on top. Add a few grinds of pepper and the remaining thyme leaves. Drizzle with white truffle oil if you wish and serve.

ROASTED CARROT FALAFEL SALAD

Serves 6

ACTIVE TIME
20 minutes

CHILLING TIME
20 minutes

COOKING TIME
50 minutes

INGREDIENTS
1 bunch carrots, preferably
   organic
2 cloves garlic, peeled
Extra-virgin olive oil
1 can (15 oz./400 g) chickpeas
2 tbsp cumin seeds
4 sprigs fresh cilantro
Finely grated zest of 1 lemon,
   preferably organic
5 tbsp all-purpose flour
10½ oz. (300 g) baby salad greens
1 red onion, thinly sliced
1 cucumber, diced
5¼ oz. (150 g) cherry tomatoes,
   halved

10½ oz. (300 g) feta, crumbled
Finely grated zest of 1 orange,
   preferably organic,
A few pickled radish slices
1 handful toasted pumpkin seeds
6 pinches gomashio (sesame
   seasoning)
3 sprigs fresh flat-leaf parsley,
   chopped
Fleur de sel
Freshly ground pepper

FOR THE TAHINI DRESSING
3 tbsp tahini
Juice of 1 lemon
Juice of 1 orange

1. Preheat the oven to 400°F (200°C/Gas mark 6). Wash and slice the carrots and place on a parchment-lined baking sheet with the garlic. Drizzle with olive oil, season with salt, and toss to coat. Bake for 30 minutes, until the carrots are tender and nicely browned.
2. Drain the chickpeas, reserving half the liquid (about ¼ cup/60 ml). Place the chickpeas and liquid in a blender with the roasted carrots and garlic, cumin seeds, and cilantro. Blend until well combined but not pureed. Taste for seasoning.
3. Transfer the falafel mixture to a large bowl and stir in the lemon zest and flour.
4. Shape the mixture into balls with a diameter of 2½–2¾ inches (6–7 cm), adding a little more flour as needed if the balls are too sticky. Place on a baking sheet, flatten slightly, and chill in the refrigerator for about 20 minutes. Preheat the oven to 375°F (190°C/Gas Mark 5), then bake the falafels for 20 minutes, until golden brown.
5. To prepare the tahini dressing, whisk the tahini, lemon juice, and orange juice together in a bowl, adding a little water if you want a thinner consistency. Season with salt and pepper.
6. Divide the salad greens among 6 serving plates and top with the falafels, red onion, cucumber, and cherry tomatoes. Sprinkle with the feta, orange zest, pickled radishes, pumpkin seeds, parsley, and gomashio. Drizzle with the tahini dressing and serve.

MAIN DISHES

ONION QUICHE

Serves 4–6

ACTIVE TIME
20 minutes

CHILLING TIME
30 minutes

COOKING TIME
45 minutes

INGREDIENTS
1 quantity savory pastry dough with thyme
 (see recipe p. 25)
7 onions (a mix of yellow and red), thinly sliced
1 tbsp butter, plus more for greasing the pan
3 tbsp Dijon mustard
2 eggs
¾ cup (200 ml) heavy cream
2 pinches ground cumin
1 handful grated Gruyère cheese
Kosher salt
Freshly ground pepper

1. Prepare the savory pastry dough with thyme leaves as indicated on page 25. Cover in plastic wrap and chill in the refrigerator for at least 30 minutes.
2. Meanwhile, place the onions in a large saucepan or Dutch oven with the butter, a generous pinch of salt, and a few grinds of pepper. Cook over medium-low heat, stirring often, until the onions are tender and translucent.
3. Preheat the oven to 350°F (180°C/Gas Mark 4) and grease an 11-inch (28-cm) tart pan or dish with butter. Roll the dough into an approximately 13-inch (32-cm) round (see Kitchen Notes). Ease the dough into the pan, gently pressing it into the sides. Trim any excess dough, prick the base with a fork, and pre-bake for 10 minutes.
4. Remove the crust from the oven and spread the mustard over the base in a thin layer. Distribute two-thirds of the onions evenly over the mustard.
5. In a bowl, beat the eggs, then whisk in the cream and cumin. Season with salt and pepper. Pour over the onions in the tart crust and sprinkle with the grated Gruyère. Scatter the remaining onions over the top and bake for 35–40 minutes, until the filling is set and the crust is golden.

KITCHEN NOTES: The easiest way to roll out the dough is between two sheets of wax paper lightly dusted with flour or parchment paper. To transfer the dough to the pan, peel off the top wax paper sheet, turn the dough over, and ease it into the pan without stretching it. Remove the second wax paper sheet and gently press the dough into the sides of the pan.

SUNDAY LUNCH ROAST CHICKEN

Serves 4–6

ACTIVE TIME
20 minutes

COOKING TIME
1 hour 40 minutes

INGREDIENTS
3 lemons, preferably organic, divided
1 whole chicken (about 4 lb./1.7 kg),
   preferably organic
Extra-virgin olive oil
A few sprigs fresh thyme
A few sprigs fresh rosemary
1 head garlic
Kosher salt
Freshly ground pepper

1. Cook 1 whole lemon in a small saucepan filled with boiling water for 10 minutes.
2. Meanwhile, massage the chicken with a little olive oil for 5 minutes. Squeeze the juice of 1 lemon all over the chicken and season with kosher salt and pepper.
3. Drain the cooked lemon and make several incisions in it with a paring knife. Place in the cavity of the chicken.
4. Wash the thyme and rosemary sprigs and place inside the chicken with the lemon.
5. Cut the head of garlic in two horizontally and place one of the halves inside the chicken.
6. Preheat the oven to 430°F (220°C/Gas Mark 7).
7. Finely slice the third lemon and use to line the base of a roasting pan or baking dish. Set the chicken with the breast side up over the lemon slices. If you wish, scatter the remaining garlic cloves around the dish. Roast the chicken for 20 minutes, then carefully turn it over and roast for another 20 minutes breast-side down. Turn the chicken over again to its original position and baste it with the pan juices. Lower the oven temperature to 350°F (180°C/Gas Mark 4) and roast the chicken for an additional 50 minutes, basting it every 20–25 minutes (2–3 times in total), until the skin is golden brown and the juices run clear when you pierce the thickest part of the thigh.
8. When the chicken is ready, lower the oven temperature to 200°F (100°C/Gas Mark ¼), cover the chicken with aluminum foil, and place it back in the oven for 15 minutes (or until you are ready to serve it), so the juices can run back into the flesh, making it succulent and easier to carve. Drizzle with the pan juices before carving.

HERB-INFUSED MASHED POTATO GRATIN

Serves 10 (as a side dish)

ACTIVE TIME
25 minutes

COOKING TIME
30 minutes

INFUSING TIME
20 minutes

INGREDIENTS
1¼ cups (300 ml) crème fraîche
1¼ cups (300 ml) whole milk
2 sticks plus 1 tbsp (8½ oz./240 g) unsalted
　butter, divided
3 sprigs fresh rosemary
2 sprigs fresh sage or thyme
2 cloves garlic, peeled
4½ lb. (2.2 kg) floury potatoes, peeled and cut
　into even-sized chunks
Salt and freshly ground pepper

1. In a saucepan, combine the crème fraîche, milk, and 2 sticks (7¾ oz./220 g) butter with the rosemary, sage, and garlic. Bring to a simmer for 2 minutes, remove from the heat, and let infuse for 15–20 minutes.

2. Meanwhile, place the potatoes in a large pan and cover them with water. Add a generous pinch of salt, bring to a boil, and cook for about 20 minutes, until the potatoes are tender. Drain and mash with a potato masher, ricer, or food mill.

3. Remove the herbs and garlic from the cream mixture and pour over the mashed potatoes. Season with salt and pepper and stir to blend.

4. Preheat the broiler and transfer the mashed potatoes to a flameproof casserole or baking dish with a depth of at least 2 inches (5 cm). With the back of a large spoon, smooth the top and make a design of your choice.

5. Melt the remaining 1 tablespoon (20 g) butter and drizzle over the potatoes. Place under the broiler for 8–10 minutes, until the potatoes are nicely browned. Serve hot.

BULGUR SALAD
WITH ZUCCHINI, AVOCADO,
AND HAZELNUTS

Serves 4

ACTIVE TIME
10 minutes

COOKING TIME
20 minutes

INGREDIENTS
1½ cups (7 oz./200 g) bulgur
Extra-virgin olive oil
3 shallots, thinly sliced
2 zucchini, diced small
3 tbsp sesame seeds
3 tbsp chopped hazelnuts
Juice of 1 lemon, preferably organic
2 tbsp thyme and rosemary-infused olive oil
   (see recipe p. 28)
1 avocado, sliced
Leaves of 3 sprigs fresh basil, chopped
Salt and freshly ground pepper

1. Bring a saucepan of salted water to a boil, add the bulgur, and cook for 10 minutes. Drain, place in a large bowl, and add a drizzle of olive oil. Stir and set aside.
2. Cook the shallots in a large skillet over medium-low heat with a small amount of olive oil and salt until very soft and translucent, stirring frequently. Add the zucchini and cook until lightly browned.
3. Reduce the heat and stir in the bulgur, sesame seeds, and hazelnuts. Cook gently for about 5 minutes, stirring often, to heat through and allow the flavors to meld.
4. Just before serving, add the lemon juice, infused oil, and salt and pepper to taste. Toss gently to combine. Arrange the avocado slices over the salad and sprinkle with the basil. Serve warm or at room temperature.

MUSHROOM AND WILD GARLIC GALETTE

Serves 6

ACTIVE TIME
25 minutes

COOKING TIME
50 minutes

INGREDIENTS
1 quantity savory pastry dough
    (see recipe p. 25 and method below)
2 tsp pink peppercorns
Scant ⅔ cup (2 oz./60 g) grated Parmesan
Leaves of 3 sprigs fresh tarragon, finely chopped
1 lb. (500 g) assorted mushrooms (shiitakes,
    chanterelles, porcini mushrooms, etc.)
4 shoots wild garlic (see Kitchen Notes)
1 tbsp unsalted butter
2 leeks, white parts only, thinly sliced
2 shallots, thinly sliced
¾ cup (200 ml) crème fraîche
Salt and freshly ground pepper

1. Prepare the savory pastry dough as indicated on page 25, adding the pink peppercorns, Parmesan, and tarragon along with the flour. Chill in the refrigerator for at least 30 minutes.
2. Meanwhile, preheat the oven to 350°F (180°C/Gas Mark 4). Clean the mushrooms and cut them into pieces, then chop the wild garlic, reserving any flowers for garnish.
3. Melt the butter in a skillet over medium-low heat and add the shallots and leeks. Cook, stirring often, until very soft. Add the mushrooms and cook for 5-7 minutes, then add the wild garlic.
4. Stir in the crème fraîche, season with salt and pepper, and remove from the heat.
5. Roll the dough into an approximately 12-inch (30-cm) round and top with the mushroom mixture, leaving a border of 2–2¾ inches (5-7 cm). Fold the edges of the dough over the filling, overlapping as you go, and bake for 40 minutes, until the crust is deeply golden. If you have wild garlic flowers, arrange them over the galette before serving.

KITCHEN NOTES: If you can't find wild garlic, use ramps, green garlic, or garlic scapes.

GREAT-AUNT GINETTE'S STUFFED CABBAGE LEAVES

Serves 6

ACTIVE TIME
20 minutes

COOKING TIME
1 hour 40 minutes

INGREDIENTS
3 shallots, finely
  chopped
4 cloves garlic, finely
  chopped

Extra-virgin olive oil
2 oz. (50 g) white or country bread
  (with the crust removed), cut
  into chunks
1 cup (250 ml) milk
1½ lb. (700 g) sausage with the
  casings removed (or a blend
  of ground meats like beef and
  pork shoulder and belly)
1 egg, lightly beaten
2 tbsp finely chopped fresh
  parsley
2 tbsp finely chopped
  fresh chives

1 tsp dried thyme
2 tsp quatre-épices spice mix
1 tsp ground cumin
½ tsp ground cloves
1 large head of cabbage
4 tbsp (2 oz./60 g) unsalted butter,
  divided
1 onion, thinly sliced
1 carrot, peeled and thinly sliced
1 bouquet garni
¾ cup (200 ml) broth (vegetable
  or chicken)
Salt and freshly ground pepper

1. For the stuffing, cook the shallots and garlic in a skillet over low heat with a little olive oil and a generous pinch of salt until very soft. In a bowl, soak the bread in the milk until it is nearly falling apart. In a large bowl, combine the sausage with the shallot-garlic mixture, the soaked bread with the milk, and the egg. Gently stir in the parsley, chives, thyme, quatre-épices, cumin, and cloves and season with salt and pepper. Chill for 15–25 minutes to let the flavors develop.

2. Remove several large outer leaves from the head of cabbage. Blanch 12 of the most attractive leaves in a large pan of boiling water for 10 minutes, then plunge them into a bowl of ice water. Drain and let cool for several minutes.

3. Set the leaves on a cutting board and place a mound of stuffing in the center of each. Fold the leaves around the stuffing to enclose it completely and tie up with kitchen twine so the parcels remain intact during cooking.

4. Melt 3 tablespoons (1¾ oz./50 g) of the butter in a Dutch oven over medium-low heat. Add the onion and carrot, and cook until softened. Carefully place the stuffed cabbage leaves in the pot, pour in the broth, and season with salt and pepper. Cover and simmer over low heat for 1–1¼ hours, regularly spooning broth over the leaves.

5. Transfer the broth to a bowl. Add the remaining butter to the pan, increase the heat slightly, and gently caramelize the stuffed cabbage leaves on both sides, taking care when turning them over. Serve with the broth.

BUTTERNUT SQUASH, ASPARAGUS, AND PEA LASAGNA

Serves 6–8

ACTIVE TIME
15 minutes

COOKING TIME
1 hour 20 minutes

INGREDIENTS
½ butternut squash
  (or pumpkin)
Extra-virgin olive oil
1 tbsp honey
1 tsp ground cinnamon
1 tsp finely chopped fresh sage
  leaves
2 yellow onions, thinly sliced
1¾ cups (8¾ oz./250 g) fresh
  green peas
2 bunches thin asparagus, ends
  trimmed, cut into pieces
1¼ cups (10½ oz./300 g) ricotta
12 oven-ready lasagna noodles
  (no pre-cooking needed)
1¼ cups (4¼ oz./120 g) grated
  Parmesan
3½ oz. (100 g) fresh arugula
2 balls burrata cheese (about
  8 oz./250 g each), cut into pieces
Salt and freshly ground pepper

1. Preheat the oven to 400°F (200°C/Gas Mark 6).
2. Peel and cut the butternut squash into pieces and set on a rimmed baking sheet. Drizzle with a little olive oil and the honey, and sprinkle with the cinnamon, sage, and salt to taste. Toss to coat the squash and bake for 25 minutes, until the squash is tender and lightly caramelized around the edges.
3. Meanwhile, cook the onions in a skillet with 1 tablespoon of olive oil and a pinch of salt over low heat until very soft. Remove from the heat.
4. Bring a large pan of generously salted water to a boil, add the peas and asparagus, and blanch for 4 minutes. Plunge into a bowl of ice water and drain well.
5. In a large bowl, combine the peas, asparagus, onions, and ricotta. Season with salt and pepper.
6. Process the roasted butternut squash to a thin puree in a food processor or blender, adding a little water or milk if necessary. Taste for seasoning.
7. Lower the oven temperature to 350°F (180°C/Gas Mark 4). Spread a thin layer of butternut squash puree across the base of a lasagna pan and cover with a layer of lasagna noodles. Top the pasta with a thin layer of the ricotta mixture, followed by another layer of butternut squash puree. Sprinkle with Parmesan and repeat with the remaining ingredients, ending with a layer of pasta topped with a thin layer of puree and Parmesan. Bake for 45–50 minutes.
8. Just before serving, scatter the arugula and burrata over the lasagna and season with pepper.

CHICKEN WITH RHUBARB

Serves 8

ACTIVE TIME
15 minutes

COOKING TIME
50 minutes

INGREDIENTS
2 tbsp quatre-épices spice mix
2 tsp ground turmeric
2 tsp ground cardamom
1 tsp ground cloves
1 tsp ground ginger

1 tbsp superfine sugar
8 chicken legs, preferably organic
Extra-virgin olive oil
⅓ cup (1½ oz./40 g) all-purpose flour
2 shallots, finely chopped
2 cloves garlic, finely chopped
1⅔ cups (400 ml) chicken broth
Juice of 2 oranges
3 tbsp red currant jam
2 stalks rhubarb, cut into ½-in. (1-cm) pieces
1 tbsp unsalted butter
Leaves of 5 sprigs fresh cilantro
Salt and freshly ground pepper

1. Preheat the oven to 350°F (180°C/Gas Mark 4).
2. In a large bowl, combine the quatre-épices, turmeric, cardamom, cloves, ginger, and sugar with a generous pinch of salt and pepper.
3. Place the chicken legs in the bowl and rub them all over with the spices.
4. Heat a small amount of olive oil in a large skillet over medium heat. Dust the chicken legs with the flour and place 3–4 legs at a time in the skillet. Brown on both sides, 3–4 minutes per side, then set aside on a plate.
5. Place the shallots and garlic in the same skillet you used for the chicken and cook for 2 minutes, stirring constantly, until browned. Add the broth, orange juice, and red currant jam and bring to a boil; cook for 2–3 minutes, allowing the sauce to reduce slightly.
6. Transfer the sauce to a baking dish and add the chicken legs. Cover with aluminum foil and bake for 35–40 minutes, until the chicken is tender.
7. Meanwhile, melt the butter in a skillet over medium heat and add the rhubarb. Cook, stirring frequently, until the rhubarb is tender but not falling apart.
8. When you remove the chicken from the oven, add the rhubarb to the baking dish. Sprinkle with the cilantro and serve.

CHERRY TOMATO PIZZA

Serves 4–6

ACTIVE TIME
7 minutes

COOKING TIME
30 minutes

INGREDIENTS
1 onion (yellow or red), chopped
4 tbsp extra-virgin olive oil, divided
1 tbsp honey
1 pint multicolored cherry tomatoes
2–3 tomatoes (a mix of medium and large),
   halved crosswise
A blend of chopped fresh herbs, such as basil,
   oregano, rosemary, and thyme
2 cloves garlic, finely chopped
1 pinch cayenne pepper
About 12 oz. (350 g) pizza dough
A few leaves fresh thyme
3 tbsp crème fraîche
1 tbsp grated Parmesan
1 ball burrata cheese (about 8 oz./250 g),
   cut into pieces
A few leaves fresh basil
Salt and freshly ground pepper

1. Preheat the oven to 410°F (210°C/Gas Mark 6).
2. In a skillet, cook the onion over medium-high heat with 1 tablespoon of the olive oil and the honey for 5 minutes, until it is just beginning to color. Season with salt and pepper, reduce the heat, and cook for an additional 5–7 minutes, until the onion is lightly caramelized.
3. Place the cherry tomatoes and larger tomatoes in a large bowl with 2 tablespoons of the olive oil, the chopped herbs, garlic, cayenne pepper, and a little salt and pepper. Gently toss to combine.
4. Stretch or roll out the pizza dough into a thin oval and sprinkle with the thyme leaves. Spread the crème fraîche over the dough, leaving a narrow border around the edge. Scatter the caramelized onions and grated Parmesan over the cream, then arrange the cherry tomatoes and tomato halves attractively on top.
5. Bake for 15 minutes, until the crust is nicely browned. Scatter the burrata and basil leaves over the hot pizza, drizzle with olive oil, and season with pepper. Serve immediately.

VEGGIE LASAGNA

Serves 6–8

ACTIVE TIME
15 minutes

COOKING TIME
1 hour 20 minutes

RESTING TIME
Overnight

INGREDIENTS
4 leeks
2 red onions, thinly sliced
Extra-virgin olive oil
10½ oz. (300 g) fresh spinach (coarse stems removed), washed thoroughly and chopped
1⅔ cups (14 oz./400 g) ricotta
4 cups (1 L) tomato sauce
12 oven-ready lasagna noodles (no pre-cooking needed)
1½ cups (5¼ oz./150 g) grated Parmesan
1 ball burrata cheese (about 8 oz./250 g), cut into pieces
2 oz. (60 g) fresh arugula
A few leaves fresh basil, chopped
1 handful shaved Parmesan
Salt and freshly ground pepper

1. Preheat the oven to 350°F (180°C/Gas Mark 4).
2. Thinly slice and wash the white and light green parts of the leeks.
3. Heat a large skillet with a drizzle of olive oil over medium-low heat. Add the leeks and onions, and cook for about 10 minutes, until softened.
4. Add the spinach and cook for an additional 3–4 minutes, until wilted.
5. Remove from the heat and let cool for 5 minutes, then stir in the ricotta. Season with salt and pepper.
6. Spread one-third of the tomato sauce across the base of a lasagna pan.
7. Cover the tomato sauce with a layer of lasagna noodles, spread half of the ricotta mixture over the pasta, and sprinkle with grated Parmesan. Repeat this layering one time with another third of the tomato sauce, a layer of pasta, the remaining ricotta mixture, and a sprinkling of Parmesan. Cover with half of the remaining tomato sauce and a final layer of pasta. Finish with the rest of the tomato sauce and Parmesan and bake for 40 minutes.
8. Let the lasagna cool completely, then cover it and place it in the refrigerator overnight to let the flavors develop.
9. To reheat the lasagna, preheat the oven to 300°F (150°C/Gas Mark 2). Cover with aluminum foil and place in the oven for 25–30 minutes, until heated through.
10. Just before serving, scatter the burrata, arugula, basil, and shaved Parmesan over the lasagna. Serve hot.

KITCHEN NOTES: Instead of plain tomato sauce, you can blend half and half with another sauce, such as cherry tomato or tomato-basil, or mix with 2 tbsp sundried tomato pesto.

GRILLED CEDAR-PLANK SALMON

Serves 6–7

ACTIVE TIME
10 minutes

SOAKING TIME
1 hour

COOKING TIME
25 minutes

INGREDIENTS
2 food-grade cedar planks for grilling
2 tbsp extra-virgin olive oil
2 tbsp granulated cane sugar
2 tbsp soy sauce
2 tbsp minced fresh ginger
2¾ lb. (1.2 kg) salmon fillets, preferably organic
    or wild-caught, skin on
3 scallions, thinly sliced
Fleur de sel
Freshly ground pepper

1. Soak the cedar planks in water for at least 1 hour, keeping them submerged.
2. In a bowl, combine the olive oil, sugar, soy sauce, and ginger to make a glaze.
3. Prepare your grill for direct cooking over medium heat. Brush the glaze evenly over the salmon.
4. Set the soaked planks on the grill for a few minutes, until they begin to smoke, adding water if they seem too dry. Place the salmon fillets skin side down on the planks, sprinkle with fleur de sel, and close the lid of the grill. Cook for 15–20 minutes, checking often, until the salmon is done to your liking. If necessary, cook for an additional 10 minutes or so.
5. Place the salmon on a serving plate, sprinkle with the scallions, and season with pepper. Serve immediately.

SUNNY EGGS BENEDICT

Serves 5

ACTIVE TIME
10 minutes

COOKING TIME
5 minutes

INGREDIENTS
5 slices multigrain bread
5 eggs
1 tbsp distilled white vinegar
1 pink grapefruit
5 thick slices smoked salmon, preferably
 wild-caught
1 handful baby salad greens
½ bunch fresh basil
Salt and freshly ground pepper

FOR THE HOLLANDAISE SAUCE
3 egg yolks
Juice of 1 lemon
1 pinch cayenne pepper
½ cup (125 ml) melted butter
1 generous tbsp all-purpose flour (if necessary)
A few leaves fresh basil, roughly chopped,
 for garnish

1. Toast the bread and set aside.
2. Fill a saucepan with water, stir in the vinegar, and bring to a boil. Lower the heat to a gentle simmer and poach the eggs for 3 minutes, lifting them out with a slotted spoon when they are ready.
3. Carefully peel the grapefruit, removing all the white pith. Cut out the grapefruit segments and slice them thinly.
4. To make the hollandaise sauce, whisk the egg yolks, lemon juice, and cayenne pepper together for about 20 seconds, using an electric beater. Slowly drizzle in the melted butter, whisking nonstop, until the sauce doubles in volume. If the sauce is too runny, whisk in the flour.
5. Place a slice of salmon on each piece of toast and sprinkle baby salad greens on top. Gently set the poached eggs over the greens and spoon the sauce over the eggs. Add the grapefruit slices and basil, season with salt and pepper, and serve.

ROASTED TOMATO AND SHALLOT TARTE TATIN

Serves 6

ACTIVE TIME

15 minutes

COOKING TIME

3 hours 40 minutes

RESTING TIME

40 minutes

INGREDIENTS

1¾ lb. (800 g) assorted tomatoes (different colors and sizes), washed and halved crosswise

Extra-virgin olive oil

2 cups (9 oz./250 g) all-purpose flour

1 stick plus 2 tbsp (5¼ oz./150 g) lightly salted butter, well chilled and diced

3 tbsp grated Parmesan

2 eggs, divided

1 tbsp (20 g) unsalted butter, for greasing the pan

5 large shallots, thinly sliced

1 tsp wine vinegar

2 tbsp honey

Leaves of 1 small bunch fresh oregano

Scant ½ cup (1¾ oz./50 g) jarred capers, drained

Salt and freshly ground pepper

1. Preheat the oven to 200°F (100°C/Gas Mark ¼). Place the tomatoes on a rimmed baking sheet, season with salt and pepper, and drizzle with olive oil. Slowly roast for 3 hours, checking occasionally, until the tomatoes are soft and wrinkled but still juicy.

2. To make the dough, combine the flour, lightly salted butter, Parmesan, and 1 egg in a bowl, until the mixture just comes together in a ball. Flatten into a disk, cover with plastic wrap, and chill in the refrigerator for 30 minutes.

3. In a large saucepan or Dutch oven, cook the shallots with a drizzle of olive oil over low heat for about 15 minutes, until very soft. Stir in the vinegar, honey, oregano, and salt and pepper to taste. Continue cooking for 15 minutes, until the shallots are lightly caramelized.

4. Preheat the oven to 400°F (200°C/Gas Mark 6) and grease an 11-inch (28-cm) tart pan or dish with the unsalted butter. Arrange the tomatoes cut-side down in the pan and scatter the shallots on top.

5. Roll the dough into an approximately 13-inch (32-cm) round. Gently lay the dough over the tomatoes and shallots and tuck the edges of the dough inside the pan. Lightly beat the remaining egg and brush over the dough. Bake for 25 minutes, until golden.

6. Fry the capers in a skillet over high heat with a little olive oil for 1–2 minutes. Place on paper towel to absorb excess grease.

7. Let the tart cool for about 10 minutes, then run a knife around the edge to release from the sides of the pan. Place a serving plate with a rim on top of the tart and upturn the tart onto the plate. Carefully lift off the pan and sprinkle the tart with the capers and fresh oregano leaves.

HERB AND WILDFLOWER-STUFFED TROUT

Serves 6

ACTIVE TIME
15 minutes

COOKING TIME
30 minutes

INGREDIENTS
2–3 large whole trout, cleaned by your
  fishmonger
3 slices preserved lemons (see recipe p. 31),
  finely chopped
3 tbsp grated fresh ginger
2 tbsp coriander seeds
A few sprigs fresh thyme
A few sprigs fresh rosemary (with flowers
  if possible)
Extra-virgin olive oil
1 lemon, preferably organic, thickly sliced
A few fresh herb sprigs, for garnish
A few edible wildflowers, for garnish
Freshly ground pepper

1. Preheat the oven to 375°F (190°C/Gas Mark 5).
2. Place the trout on a rimmed baking sheet lined with parchment paper.
3. In a bowl, combine the preserved lemons, ginger, and coriander seeds with a drizzle of olive oil and a few grinds of pepper (the preserved lemons provide plenty of salt).
4. Stuff the trout with the preserved lemon mixture, lay a few thyme and rosemary sprigs on top of each fish, and tie with the twine to keep the stuffing inside and the herbs in place.
5. Drizzle the trout with olive oil. Distribute the fresh lemon slices around the fish.
6. Bake for 30 minutes, until the fish is opaque and gently flakes apart when tested with the tip of a knife.
7. Before serving, garnish with a few fresh herb sprigs and wildflowers.

IMPROVISED SUNDAY FRITTATA

Serves 5-6

ACTIVE TIME
15 minutes

COOKING TIME
30 minutes

INGREDIENTS
10 or so small potatoes, such as Cheyenne or another waxy, thin-skinned variety

Extra-virgin olive oil
1 leek, white part only, cut into 4 pieces
1 yellow onion, chopped
2 green scallion tops, finely chopped
3½ oz. (100 g) baby spinach
⅔ cup (3½ oz./100 g) fresh green peas
⅔ cup (3½ oz./100 g) shelled fava beans
10 eggs
3 tbsp crème fraîche

⅔ cup (3½ oz./100 g) feta or fresh goat cheese, crumbled
A few fresh chives, finely chopped, plus chive flowers for garnish
A few leaves fresh parsley, finely chopped
A few sprigs fresh dill, finely chopped
Finely grated zest of 1 lemon, preferably organic
Kosher salt
Freshly ground pepper

1. Cook the potatoes in a large pan of boiling salted water for about 15 minutes. Drain and set aside.
2. Heat a small amount of olive oil in a large oven-safe skillet (preferably cast-iron) over medium heat. Add the leek, yellow onion, scallion tops, and a little salt. Cook until softened.
3. Thinly slice the potatoes, leaving the skin on. Add to the skillet and reduce the heat slightly.
4. Add the baby spinach and cook for 3–4 minutes, until wilted. Gently stir in the peas and fava beans and remove from the heat.
5. In a bowl, whisk the eggs with the crème fraîche and season with salt and pepper. Pour over the vegetables in the skillet, increase the heat slightly, and cook for 5–7 minutes, letting the eggs slowly set.
6. Preheat the oven to 350°F (180°C/Gas Mark 4).
7. Sprinkle the feta over the skillet and place in the oven for 5–6 minutes, until the top is set and the cheese is partially melted.
8. Remove from the oven and sprinkle with the chives, chive flowers, parsley, dill, and lemon zest. This dish is equally good served hot or cold.

KITCHEN NOTES: This dish lends itself to variation, so feel free to improvise according to the season or the vegetables you have on hand.

BAKED CHICKEN AND PEACHES

Serves 5

ACTIVE TIME
15 minutes

COOKING TIME
45 minutes

INGREDIENTS
Extra-virgin olive oil
5 chicken legs, preferably organic
2 red onions, quartered
5 peaches (a mix of yellow and white), quartered
Juice of 1 orange, preferably organic
Leaves of 3 sprigs fresh tarragon
Fleur de sel
Freshly ground pepper

1. Preheat the oven to 400°F (200°C/Gas Mark 6).
2. Heat a small amount of olive oil in a large skillet over high heat. Brown the chicken legs in the skillet for 3–4 minutes on both sides. Transfer to a baking dish.
3. Add the onions to the baking dish.
4. Tuck the peaches in between the chicken legs and drizzle everything with a little olive oil and the orange juice. Season with fleur de sel and pepper and bake for 40–45 minutes. If the chicken is not quite cooked through, lower the oven temperature to 350°F (180°C/Gas Mark 4) and bake for an additional 10 minutes or so, depending on the size of the legs.
5. Sprinkle with the tarragon leaves before serving.

EGGPLANT, ZUCCHINI, AND LEMON PIZZA WITH ZA'ATAR

Serves 6

ACTIVE TIME
10 minutes

COOKING TIME
30 minutes

INGREDIENTS
About 12 oz. (350 g) pizza dough
2 lemons, preferably organic
2 small eggplants, thinly sliced
3 small zucchini, thinly sliced
3 tbsp extra-virgin olive oil
7 oz. (200 g) feta, sliced
Za'atar, for sprinkling (see recipe p. 27)

1. Preheat the oven to 400°F (200°C/Gas Mark 6). Stretch or roll out the pizza dough into a thin oval and set on a baking sheet.
2. Thinly slice one of the lemons and place in a large bowl with the sliced eggplants and zucchini. Add the juice of the remaining lemon and the olive oil and toss to coat.
3. Arrange the feta in a thin layer over the pizza dough, leaving a narrow border. Distribute the eggplant, zucchini, and lemon slices evenly over the cheese, then sprinkle with za'atar. Bake for 30 minutes, until the crust and vegetables are lightly golden.

COUNTRY-STYLE VEAL

Serves 5–6

ACTIVE TIME
10 minutes

COOKING TIME
50 minutes

INGREDIENTS

2¼ lb. (1 kg) boneless veal rump or shoulder
1¾ lb. (800 g) assorted mushrooms (porcini, shiitakes, girolles, etc.)
2 tbsp extra-virgin olive oil
3 tbsp. (1¾ oz./50 g) lightly salted butter
2 shallots, thinly sliced
¾ cup (200 ml) broth (vegetable or chicken)
12 baby potatoes, unpeeled and washed
2 sprigs fresh thyme
¾ cup (3½ oz./100 g) toasted hazelnuts
3 tbsp crème fraîche
Cooked rice of your choice, for serving
Salt and freshly ground pepper

1. Cut the veal into medium-sized pieces. Clean the mushrooms and cut them into halves or thirds depending on their size.
2. Heat the olive oil and butter in a Dutch oven over medium-high heat. Add the shallots and cook, stirring often, until softened.
3. Season the veal all over with fleur de sel and pepper, add it to the pan, and brown it on all sides. Stir in the mushrooms and cook until lightly browned.
4. Pour in the broth and add the potatoes and thyme sprigs. Bring to a simmer and cook, partially covered, for 20–25 minutes, or until the veal is completely tender.
5. Stir in the hazelnuts and crème fraîche and season with salt and pepper. Simmer for an additional 15 minutes over low heat. Serve with rice.

PASTA WITH SHIITAKES, ROASTED SWEET POTATO, AND SAGE

Serves 6

ACTIVE TIME
15 minutes

COOKING TIME
35 minutes

INGREDIENTS
1 large sweet potato
Leaves of 2 sprigs fresh sage, divided
4 tbsp extra-virgin olive oil, divided, plus more
  for the skillet
¾ lb. (350 g) shiitake mushrooms
2 cloves garlic, finely chopped
1 lb. (500 g) strozzapreti pasta
1½ cups (150 g) grated pecorino
Salt and freshly ground pepper

1. Preheat the oven to 410°F (210°C/Gas Mark 6) and line a rimmed baking sheet with parchment paper.
2. Peel and cut the sweet potato into small cubes and chop the leaves of 1 sage sprig. Spread the sweet potatoes out on the prepared baking sheet in a single layer. Drizzle with 2 tablespoons of the olive oil, sprinkle with salt and pepper, and gently toss with your fingers to coat each piece well.
3. Bake for 20 minutes, until the sweet potatoes are tender and lightly browned.
4. Meanwhile, clean the shiitake mushrooms and cut them into pieces. Sauté in a skillet over high heat with a little olive oil, salt, and pepper for 5–7 minutes, until golden. Transfer to a plate.
5. Just before the sweet potatoes are done, remove the baking sheet from the oven and scatter with the garlic and chopped sage leaves. Stir gently to combine, return to the oven, and bake for an additional 5 minutes.
6. Cook the pasta in boiling salted water until al dente, following the timing indicated on the package. Drain and transfer to a large serving dish.
7. Add the sweet potato, shiitake mushrooms, and the remaining 2 tablespoons of olive oil. Gently combine. Sprinkle with the remaining sage leaves, grated pecorino, and a few grinds of pepper. Serve warm or cold.

HAY-BAKED LAMB

Serves 6

ACTIVE TIME
15 minutes

COOKING TIME
1 hour 30 minutes

INGREDIENTS
9 oz. (250 g) food-grade hay, preferably organic
4 tbsp (1¾ oz./50 g) lightly salted butter,
    divided
2 tbsp extra-virgin olive oil
3½ lb. (1.5 kg) leg of lamb (with or without
    the bone)
3 carrots, sliced
3 yellow onions, thinly sliced
1 head garlic
1 lb. (500 g) baby potatoes, unpeeled
    and washed
Salt and freshly ground pepper

1. Wash the hay and gently wring out excess water. Wrap in a dish towel and set aside.
2. In a Dutch oven, melt 2 tablespoons (25 g) of the butter with the olive oil over high heat. Sear the lamb on all sides, about 5 minutes per side, seasoning it with salt and pepper as it cooks. Transfer to a cutting board.
3. Melt the remaining butter in the same pot over low heat. Add the carrots and onions and cook until softened. Transfer to a bowl.
4. Preheat the oven to 375°F (190°C/Gas Mark 5) and line the base of the Dutch oven with half of the hay.
5. Cut the head of garlic in half crosswise and place on the hay. Set the lamb in the pot and top with the carrots and onions. Cover with the remaining hay, put the lid on the pot, and bake for 50 minutes.
6. Remove from the oven and arrange the potatoes around the lamb. Return to the oven for an additional 30 minutes, until the meat and potatoes are completely tender. If necessary, bake for an additional 10–15 minutes.
7. Transfer the lamb to a serving dish, removing any hay stuck to the meat. Surround with the potatoes and garlic. Strain the flavorful pan juices and serve on the side as a delicious sauce.

RIGATONI WITH CARROT-TOP PESTO AND CARAMELIZED CARROTS

Serves 5–6

ACTIVE TIME
5 minutes

COOKING TIME
12 minutes

INGREDIENTS
1 lb. (500 g) dried rigatoni pasta
2 large carrots
Extra-virgin olive oil
1 tbsp maple syrup
4 tbsp carrot-top pesto (see recipe p. 29)
1 cup (3½ oz./100 g) shaved Parmesan
Leaves of 1 small bunch fresh basil
Salt
Crushed black pepper

1. Cook the pasta in a large pan of boiling salted water for about 12 minutes, or to your desired doneness (check the timing indicated on the package).
2. While the pasta is cooking, peel and thinly slice the carrots. Sauté in a skillet with the maple syrup and a little olive oil over medium heat until just tender and caramelized around the edges. Season with salt and pepper.
3. Before draining the pasta, set aside ½ cup of the cooking water. Drain the pasta, return to the pan, and stir in a drizzle of olive oil.
4. Add the pesto and cooking water and toss to combine. Stir in the carrots.
5. Sprinkle with the Parmesan, basil, and crushed pepper, and serve immediately.

PORK TENDERLOIN WITH APPLES

Serves 4–5

ACTIVE TIME
15 minutes

COOKING TIME
25 minutes

INGREDIENTS
1 pork tenderloin (about 1¼ lb./600 g)
½ cup (3½ oz./100 g) light brown sugar
3 tbsp Dijon mustard
3 tbsp unsweetened apple juice
3 cloves garlic. finely chopped
3 tbsp extra-virgin olive oil
2 apples. skin on. cut into ½-in. (1-cm) slices
2 sprigs fresh thyme. snipped into
   small pieces
Salt and freshly ground pepper

1. Generously season the pork with salt and pepper.
2. In a bowl, combine the brown sugar, mustard, apple juice, and garlic to make a glaze.
3. Coat the pork with the glaze and set aside the rest.
4. Heat the olive oil in a large skillet over high heat. Add the pork tenderloin and cook until golden brown all over, turning it every 2–3 minutes.
5. Place the apple slices in the pan around the pork and lower the heat to medium. Cook for 10–15 minutes, until the apples are tender and browned, occasionally turning them over.
6. Pour the remaining glaze over the pork if necessary—the meat should be deeply caramelized.
7. Sprinkle with the thyme sprigs, season with salt and pepper, and serve immediately.

DUCK AND HAZELNUT COTTAGE PIE

Serves 6

ACTIVE TIME
20 minutes

COOKING TIME
35 minutes

INGREDIENTS
1 lb. (500 g) medium-sized floury potatoes
4 confit duck legs
20 or so hazelnuts, roughly chopped
2 shallots, finely chopped
1 yellow onion, finely chopped
2 tsp quatre-épices spice mix
1 tbsp honey
2 cups (500 ml) crème fraîche
3 tbsp (1¾ oz./50 g) unsalted butter, softened,
    plus 2 tbsp (1 oz./25 g) firm butter, cut into
    small pieces
Leaves of 3 sprigs fresh thyme
1 tsp ground nutmeg
Salt and freshly ground pepper

1. Wash the potatoes and cook them unpeeled and whole in a large pan of boiling salted water, until tender all the way through (the time will depend on their size).
2. Preheat the oven to 350°F (180°C/Gas Mark 4).
3. Remove the meat from the duck legs and shred it into a large bowl. Stir in the hazelnuts, shallots, onion, quatre-épices, and honey. Cook this mixture in a skillet over low heat for 10 minutes, until fragrant and browning in places. Season with salt and pepper.
4. Peel the potatoes and mash them with a fork. Mash in the crème fraîche, softened butter, thyme, and nutmeg.
5. Spread one-third of the duck mixture over the base of a 2-quart (2-L) casserole or baking dish.
6. Combine the remaining duck mixture with half of the mashed potatoes and spread over the duck layer. Cover with an even layer of the remaining potatoes, then scatter the pieces of butter over the top. Season with a few grinds of pepper and bake for 25 minutes, until the filling is bubbling and the potatoes are golden brown.

BUTTERNUT SQUASH AND SAGE GALETTE

Serves 5

ACTIVE TIME
25 minutes

COOKING TIME
40 minutes

CHILLING TIME
30 minutes

INGREDIENTS
1 quantity savory pastry dough
  (see recipe p. 25 and method below)
Leaves of 1 bunch fresh sage, chopped
  (reserve 2–3 leaves for garnish)
1 butternut squash
Extra-virgin olive oil
2 shallots, thinly sliced
5¼ oz. (150 g) fresh goat cheese
Salt and freshly ground pepper

1. Preheat the oven to 400°F (200°C/Gas Mark 6).
2. Prepare the pastry dough, adding 2 tablespoons chopped sage leaves along with the flour. Chill in the refrigerator for 30 minutes.
3. Meanwhile, peel the butternut squash, scoop out the seeds, and cut the flesh into thin slices. Place on a baking sheet, drizzle with oil, and sprinkle with salt, pepper, and 2 tablespoons sage leaves. Toss to coat. Bake for 15 minutes, until the squash is tender and lightly browned around the edges.
4. Brown the shallots in a large skillet with a drizzle of olive oil over medium heat. Remove from the heat.
5. Add the butternut squash and goat cheese to the skillet with the shallots and gently combine.
6. Lower the oven temperature to 350°F (180°C/Gas Mark 4).
7. Roll the dough into an approximately 12-inch (30-cm) round and top with the butternut squash mixture, leaving a border of 2–2¾ inches (5–7 cm). Fold the edges of the dough over the filling, overlapping slightly as you go. Bake for 25 minutes, until the crust is crisp and golden brown.
8. Remove the galette from the oven and let it rest for about 10 minutes. Top with 2 or 3 sage leaves and serve.

See photo pp. 170–71

CARAMELIZED ONION AND APPLE TART

Serves 6–8

ACTIVE TIME
15 minutes

COOKING TIME
35 minutes

INGREDIENTS
3 medium yellow onions, thinly sliced
3 tbsp extra-virgin olive oil
1 tbsp honey
2 red apples, skin on, cored and thinly sliced
1 sheet ready-rolled puff pastry
4 tbsp crème fraîche
Leaves of 3 sprigs fresh thyme
Salt and freshly ground pepper

1. Preheat the oven to 400°F (200°C/Gas Mark 6).
2. Heat the olive oil in a large skillet over medium heat. Add the onions and a generous pinch of salt and stir to combine. Stir in the honey and cook for 7–8 minutes, stirring often, until the onions are lightly caramelized. Stir in the apples and cook for an additional 5 minutes.
3. Trim the puff pastry into a rectangle measuring about 12 × 8 inches (30 × 20 cm) and place on a baking sheet. Spread the crème fraîche over the pastry, leaving a narrow border. Scatter the onions and apples evenly over the crème fraîche and bake for 20–25 minutes, until the crust is golden. Sprinkle with thyme and pepper, cut into squares, and serve.

See photo pp. 170–71

PORK CHOPS WITH FRESH APRICOTS AND APRICOT CHUTNEY

Serves 4

ACTIVE TIME
5 minutes

COOKING TIME
25 minutes

INGREDIENTS
Extra-virgin olive oil
1 large white onion, thinly sliced
4 pork chops
4 fresh apricots, halved
2 sprigs fresh rosemary, cut into small pieces
Apricot chutney (see recipe p. 30)
Salt and freshly ground pepper

1. Heat a drizzle of olive oil in a large cast-iron skillet over medium heat. Add the onion and a pinch of salt and cook until softened.
2. Season the pork chops with salt, place in the skillet with the onions, and brown on both sides. Lower the heat and add the fresh apricots and rosemary sprigs to the pan.
3. When the pork chops are cooked to your liking and the apricots are very soft, divide the meat, fruit, and onions among four serving plates. Raise the heat under the skillet to reduce the pan juices slightly, then drizzle over the pork chops. Serve immediately with the apricot chutney on the side.

APPLE-STUFFED SPAGHETTI SQUASH

Serves 6

ACTIVE TIME
20 minutes

COOKING TIME
1 hour

INGREDIENTS
3 medium spaghetti squash
4 tbsp extra-virgin olive oil, divided
1 cup (6½ oz./180 g) basmati rice

2 small yellow onions, thinly sliced
2 apples (such as Belle de Boskoop), peeled, cored, and cut into small pieces
7 oz. (200 g) fresh spinach (coarse stems removed), washed thoroughly and roughly chopped
1 tsp dried sage
1 tsp dried oregano
1 handful dried cranberries
1 handful toasted pumpkin seeds
Zest of 1 lemon, preferably organic (optional)
Salt and freshly ground pepper

1. Preheat the oven to 410°F (210°C/Gas Mark 6) and line a baking sheet with aluminum foil.
2. Wash the spaghetti squash and cut in half lengthwise. Scoop out the seeds and a bit of the flesh to make a hollow for the filling. Brush the cut side of the squash with 2 tablespoons of the olive oil and sprinkle with salt. Place cut side down on the prepared baking sheet and bake for 25 minutes.
3. Meanwhile, cook the rice in a saucepan of simmering salted water for 15 minutes or until tender. Drain and place in a large bowl.
4. Sauté the onions in a hot skillet with the remaining 2 tablespoons of olive oil for 3–4 minutes.
5. Add the apples and cook for an additional 5 minutes, until just tender.
6. Stir in the spinach and cook until wilted, then season with salt and pepper. Transfer to the bowl with the rice and stir to combine.
7. Add the sage, oregano, cranberries, pumpkin seeds, and lemon zest if you are using it. Taste and adjust the seasoning if necessary.
8. Remove the baking sheet from the oven, turn the squash over, and fill the cavities with the rice mixture.
9. Lower the oven temperature to 350°F (180°C/Gas Mark 4) and bake the stuffed squash for 10 minutes, until heated through. Serve hot.

ROAST TURKEY WITH CLEMENTINES AND GARLIC

Serves 10

ACTIVE TIME
15 minutes

RESTING TIME
1 hour minimum
(preferably overnight)

COOKING TIME
About 2 hours 30 minutes

INGREDIENTS
10 sprigs fresh thyme, divided
5¼ oz. (150 g) unsalted butter,
softened

5 clementines, preferably organic,
zested and halved
3 cloves garlic, finely chopped
1 turkey (about 11 lb./5 kg)
2 cups (480 ml) chicken broth
6 heads garlic, divided
Salt and freshly ground pepper

1. Measure out 2 tablespoons of thyme leaves and set the remaining sprigs aside. In a bowl, combine the thyme leaves with the butter, grated clementine zest, and chopped garlic.
2. Gently slide your fingers under the turkey skin to separate the skin from the meat on the breast and legs. Rub three-quarters of the butter mixture under the skin. Spread the remaining butter mixture all over the outside of the skin and massage it in. Season the turkey with salt and pepper, set it in a roasting pan, and let it rest for at least 1 hour at room temperature.
3. Preheat the oven to 400°F (200°C/Gas Mark 6) and roast the turkey for 30 minutes, until lightly golden.
4. Carefully pour the broth into the roasting pan and roast for another 30 minutes.
5. Meanwhile, cut 5 of the garlic heads in half crosswise. When the 30 minutes are up, place the clementine halves, halved garlic heads, and the remaining thyme sprigs around the turkey in the pan. Roast for an additional 1 hour, basting every 20 minutes with the pan juices, until the skin is crisp and the turkey is cooked through (when you cut between the leg and thigh, the juices should run clear). If more time in the oven is needed, continue basting regularly.
6. Meanwhile, peel and crush the cloves of the remaining head of garlic. When the turkey is done, transfer the pan juices to a saucepan, add the garlic, and simmer for 5–7 minutes to reduce. Taste and adjust the seasoning if necessary.
7. Place the turkey on a serving dish and arrange the clementine halves and halved garlic heads around the meat. Serve with the sauce.

KITCHEN NOTES: For even better flavor, you can prepare the turkey through step 3 a day ahead and keep it in the refrigerator overnight. Be sure to remove the turkey from the fridge at least 1 hour before roasting to allow it to come to room temperature first.

DESSERTS

ORANGE BLOSSOM CAKE

Serves 8

ACTIVE TIME
15 minutes

RESTING TIME
10 minutes

COOKING TIME
45 minutes

INGREDIENTS
1 stick plus 2 tsp (4½ oz./125 g) unsalted butter, plus more for greasing the pan
⅔ cup (150 ml) whole or low-fat milk
3 eggs
1 cup (7 oz./200 g) granulated or superfine sugar, plus more for dusting
1 pinch salt
¾ cup (180 ml) + 1 generous tbsp (20 ml) orange blossom water
3¾ cups (15¾ oz./450 g) all-purpose flour
Scant 1 tbsp (11 g) baking powder
1 pinch baking soda
½ cup (125 ml) boiling water

1. Preheat the oven to 400°F (200°C/Gas Mark 6) and grease a standard loaf pan with butter.
2. Place the butter and milk in a saucepan and cook over low heat until the butter melts. Remove from the heat.
3. In a large bowl, whisk the eggs and sugar together until pale and creamy. Add the salt, ¾ cup (180 ml) orange blossom water, flour, baking powder, and baking soda. Stir until just combined.
4. Gradually add the milk-butter mixture, stirring constantly, until the batter is just smooth.
5. Pour the batter into the prepared loaf pan and let rest for about 10 minutes on the counter.
6. Bake for about 45 minutes, until the cake is risen, golden brown, and the tip of a pointed knife inserted into the center comes out clean. If necessary, bake for an additional 10–15 minutes.
7. While the cake is still hot, combine the generous tablespoon (20 ml) of orange blossom water with the boiling water and carefully drizzle over the top of the cake. Let the cake cool in the pan before turning it out onto a serving plate.
8. Dust the cake with sugar and serve.

CHERRY CLAFOUTIS

Serves 6

ACTIVE TIME
15 minutes

COOKING TIME
35 minutes

INGREDIENTS
½ cup (3½ oz./100 g) granulated sugar,
   plus a little more for the pan
4 eggs
¾ cup plus 1 tbsp (3½ oz./100 g) all-purpose
   flour
1 pinch salt
1 cup plus scant ½ cup (350 ml) whole
   or low-fat milk
2 tbsp rum
2 tbsp (1 oz./30 g) unsalted butter, melted and
   cooled, plus more for greasing the pan
1¼ lb. (600 g) cherries
Confectioners' sugar, for dusting

1. Preheat the oven to 400°F (200°C/Gas Mark 6). Grease an 11–12-inch (28–30-cm) tart pan or dish with butter and sprinkle with a little granulated sugar.
2. In a large bowl, whisk the granulated sugar and eggs together until pale and frothy.
3. Whisk in the flour, salt, and rum, followed by the melted butter. Continue whisking until smooth.
4. Wash the cherries and remove the stems (I leave the pits in, but you can remove them if you prefer). Arrange the cherries in a single layer in the base of the tart dish. Pour the batter over them and bake for 35 minutes, until the custard is set and lightly browned.
5. Just before serving, dust the clafoutis with confectioners' sugar. Serve warm, at room temperature, or cold.

KITCHEN NOTES: Feel free to swap out the cherries for different seasonal fruits, such as apples or pears in the winter or peaches, apricots, blackberries, or raspberries in the spring or summer. Prepare larger fruits, as necessary, and cut into even-size pieces.

ROASTED PINEAPPLE WITH COCONUT-RUM WHIPPED CREAM

Serves 4–5

ACTIVE TIME
15 minutes

COOKING TIME
30 minutes

INGREDIENTS
1 pineapple
Scant ½ cup (3½ oz./100 g) demerara sugar
2 tsp ground ginger
1 tbsp ground cardamom
5 tbsp (2½ oz./75 g) unsalted butter, cut into
 pieces
¾ cup (200 ml) coconut cream
3 tbsp dark rum
1 pinch sweet paprika

1. Preheat the oven to 375°F (190°C/Gas Mark 5). Peel the pineapple, keeping the top with the leaves intact, and set in a baking dish.
2. In a bowl, combine the demerara sugar, ginger, and cardamom. Coat the pineapple all over with this mixture.
3. Scatter the butter around the pineapple in the baking dish and bake for 30 minutes, turning the pineapple over halfway through the cooking time. Spoon cooking juices over the fruit from time to time to keep it moist.
4. Meanwhile, whisk the coconut cream until it thickens and holds soft peaks. Whisk in the rum. Set aside in the refrigerator until you are ready to serve the pineapple.
5. Sprinkle the paprika over the roasted pineapple and cut it into slices. Top each serving with 1 or 2 generous spoonfuls of the coconut whipped cream.

DARK CHOCOLATE COCONUT BITES

Makes 30–35

ACTIVE TIME
10 minutes

FREEZING TIME
20 minutes

INGREDIENTS
3 cups (12 oz./350 g) unsweetened shredded
 coconut
1 can (14 oz./400 g) sweetened condensed milk
9 oz. (250 g) dark chocolate, roughly chopped

1. Place the shredded coconut in a large bowl and gradually stir in the sweetened condensed milk until the mixture holds together—it should not be runny.
2. Shape the mixture into balls (about the size of a golf ball) and set on a baking sheet lined with parchment paper. Place the baking sheet in the freezer for 20 minutes.
3. Meanwhile, melt the chocolate in a bowl set over a hot water bath.
4. Using a spoon, dip each coconut ball into the melted chocolate to coat fully and return to the parchment-lined baking sheet. Place the baking sheet in the refrigerator until the chocolate sets and you are ready to serve them.

ALMOND-ORANGE BLOSSOM ICE CREAM WITH PISTACHIOS AND ROSE PETALS

Serves 6–8

ACTIVE TIME
10 minutes

COOKING TIME
20 minutes

CHILLING TIME
30 minutes

FREEZING TIME
5 hours

INGREDIENTS
3 tbsp cornstarch
1 cup plus scant ½ cup (350 ml) heavy cream
1 cup plus scant ½ cup (350 ml) unsweetened
  almond milk
¾ cup (5 oz./150 g) superfine sugar
5 tbsp orange blossom water
Generous ⅓ cup (1¾ oz./50 g) shelled unsalted
  pistachios
A few food-grade rose petals (not treated
  with pesticides)

1. Combine the cornstarch and cream in a large bowl.
2. Gently heat the almond milk with the sugar in a large saucepan, stirring often, until the sugar dissolves. Add to the cornstarch-cream mixture and whisk or stir until well combined.
3. Pour this mixture back into the same saucepan and cook over low heat, stirring constantly, until thickened.
4. Remove from the heat and stir in the orange blossom water.
5. Transfer to a large bowl and set aside.
6. Cook the pistachios in a dry skillet over low heat for about 10 minutes, stirring frequently, until toasted and fragrant. Remove from the skillet, let cool slightly, then chop roughly.
7. Stir the pistachios into the cream mixture, reserving a handful for garnish.
8. Transfer the cream mixture to an airtight container and chill in the refrigerator for 30 minutes, then transfer to the freezer. Freeze for at least 5 hours.
9. Remove the ice cream from the freezer 10 minutes before serving. Scoop into bowls, sprinkle with the remaining pistachios and a few rose petals, and serve.

LEMON AND THYME CAKE

Serves 8

ACTIVE TIME
15 minutes

COOKING TIME
45 minutes

RESTING TIME
10 minutes

INGREDIENTS

FOR THE CAKE
1 stick plus 2 tsp (4½ oz./125 g) unsalted butter, plus more for greasing the pan
⅔ cup (150 ml) whole or reduced-fat milk
3 eggs
1 cup (7 oz./200 g) granulated or superfine sugar
1 pinch salt
Finely grated zest of 3 lemons, preferably organic
3¼ cups (14 oz./400 g) all-purpose flour
1 scant tbsp (11 g) baking powder
1 pinch baking soda
Leaves of 4 thyme sprigs, divided

FOR THE GLAZE
1½ cups (7 oz./200 g) confectioners' sugar
3 tbsp lemon juice

1. To make the cake, preheat the oven to 400°F (200°C/Gas Mark 6) and grease a 9-inch (23-cm) Bundt pan or savarin mold with butter.
2. Place the butter and milk in a saucepan and cook over low heat until the butter melts. Remove from the heat.
3. In a large bowl, whisk the eggs with the sugar until pale and creamy.
4. Add the salt, lemon zest, flour, baking soda, baking powder, and three-quarters of the thyme leaves. Stir until just combined.
5. Gradually add the milk-butter mixture, stirring nonstop, until the batter is just smooth.
6. Pour the batter into the prepared mold and bake for about 45 minutes, until the cake is risen and golden and the tip of a pointed knife inserted into it comes out clean. If necessary, bake for an additional 10–15 minutes.
7. Let the cake cool for about 10 minutes in the mold, then turn it out onto a serving plate and let cool completely.
8. To prepare the glaze, combine the confectioners' sugar and lemon juice in a bowl and drizzle over the cake. Garnish with the remaining thyme leaves and serve.

FRANOU'S* LEMON PIE

Serves 6–8

ACTIVE TIME
20 minutes

CHILLING TIME
2 hours

COOKING TIME
35 minutes

INGREDIENTS
FOR THE PASTRY DOUGH
1 egg yolk
½ cup (3½ oz./100 g) granulated
   or superfine sugar
3½ tbsp (50 ml) water or milk
2 cups (9 oz./250 g) all-purpose flour
1 pinch salt
1 stick plus 2 tsp (4½ oz./125 g)
   unsalted butter, well chilled
   and diced, plus more for
   greasing the pan

Generous ½ cup (3 oz./80 g)
   toasted pine nuts

FOR THE LEMON CURD FILLING
2 large lemons, preferably
   organic
1 stick plus 2 tbsp (5 oz./150 g)
   unsalted butter
⅔ cup (4½ oz./130 g) granulated
   or superfine sugar
3 small eggs

1. To prepare the pastry dough, whisk together the egg yolk and sugar in a bowl, then whisk in the milk. Combine the flour and salt in a large bowl. Add the butter and rub it into the flour with your fingertips until coarse crumbs form. Work in the egg-sugar mixture, followed by the pine nuts, until the dough just comes together in a ball. Shape into a round, flatten the top, cover with plastic wrap, and let rest in the refrigerator for 30 minutes.

2. Preheat the oven to 350°F (180°C/Gas Mark 4) and grease an 11-inch (28-cm) tart pan or dish with butter. Roll the dough into an approximately 13-inch (33-cm) round. Ease the dough into the pan, gently pressing it into the sides. Trim any excess dough, prick the base with a fork, and bake for 25 minutes, until golden. Remove from the oven and set aside.

3. To prepare the lemon curd filling, remove the zest from 1 of the lemons in strips, using a vegetable peeler; juice both lemons and set the juice aside. Bring a saucepan of water to the boil, add the zest, and blanch zest for 5 minutes. Drain the zest and return it to the saucepan. Add the butter and cook over low heat until the butter melts. Strain through a fine-mesh sieve into a bowl.

4. Meanwhile, in another bowl, whisk the sugar and eggs together. Whisk in the lemon juice, followed by the melted butter. Pour into the saucepan and set over low heat. Cook, stirring constantly with a wooden spoon, until the mixture coats the back of the spoon and has slightly thickened; this could take up to 8–10 minutes. Do not let the mixture boil or it may split. Remove from the heat and let cool for about 10 minutes. Cover and chill in the refrigerator for 1½ hours. Spoon the chilled filling into the baked crust, smooth over the top, and serve.

* Franou is my mother's nickname.

CLEMENTINE AND PISTACHIO CAKE

Serves 8–10

ACTIVE TIME
15 minutes

COOKING TIME
50 minutes

RESTING TIME
15 minutes

INGREDIENTS

FOR THE CAKE
2 clementines, preferably organic
¾ cup (5 oz./150 g) granulated
  sugar
2 tsp quatre-épices spice mix
6 whole cloves
2½ cups (10½ oz./300 g) all-
  purpose flour
1 scant tbsp (11 g) baking powder
1 pinch baking soda
1 pinch salt
3 eggs

1¾ sticks (7 oz./200 g) unsalted
  butter, melted and cooled, plus
  more for greasing the pan
⅔ cup (150 ml) milk
½ cup (2 oz./60 g) toasted shelled
  pistachios, roughly chopped,
  plus a small handful for garnish

FOR THE GLAZE
2 clementines, preferably organic
1½ cups (7 oz./200 g)
  confectioners' sugar

1. To make the cake, finely grate the zest from one of the clementines and juice both of them. Place the zest and juice in a bowl with the granulated sugar, quatre-épices, and cloves. Stir to combine, cover, and set aside for at least 15 minutes.
2. Preheat the oven to 350°F (180°C/Gas Mark 4) and grease a standard loaf pan with butter.
3. In a large bowl, combine the flour, baking powder, baking soda, and salt.
4. In a separate bowl, lightly beat the eggs.
5. Remove the cloves from the clementine-sugar mixture and add the mixture to the eggs.
6. Add the melted butter and stir until smooth. Gently incorporate the flour mixture in several additions, then stir in the milk and pistachios until just combined.
7. Pour the batter into the prepared loaf pan and bake for 45–50 minutes, until the cake is golden brown and the tip of a pointed knife inserted into the center comes out clean.
8. Let the cake cool for about 10 minutes in the pan, then turn it out onto a cooling rack and let cool completely.
9. To make the glaze, zest one of the clementines and juice both of them. Place the zest and juice in a bowl with the confectioners' sugar and stir until smooth. If the glaze is too thin for your liking, slowly add more confectioners' sugar until you get the consistency you like.
10. When the cake has cooled, drizzle it with the glaze, sprinkle it with the pistachios, and serve.

CITRUS CAKE

Serves 6–8

ACTIVE TIME
20 minutes

COOKING TIME
40 minutes

INGREDIENTS
1 grapefruit, preferably
   organic
1 small lemon, preferably organic
2 tangerines, preferably organic
2 oranges, preferably organic
1¼ cups (8½ oz./240 g) superfine
   sugar, divided
⅓ cup (90 ml) water
1½ sticks (6 oz./180 g) unsalted
   butter, at room temperature,
   divided, plus more for greasing
   the pan
2 pinches salt
⅓ cup (2½ oz./70 g) granulated
   sugar
2 eggs
1 tsp pure vanilla extract
1⅔ cups (7 oz./200 g) all-purpose
   flour
1 tsp baking powder
1 pinch baking soda
2 tsp ground cinnamon
½ cup (4½ oz./125 g) plain whole-
   milk yogurt

1. Preheat the oven to 350°F (180°C/Gas Mark 4) and grease an 11-inch (28-cm) round cake pan with butter.
2. Wash and thinly slice the grapefruit, lemon, tangerines, and 1 orange, leaving the peel on. Cut 4 tablespoons (2 oz./60 g) of the butter into small dice.
3. Combine 1 scant cup (6 oz./170 g) of the superfine sugar with the water in a saucepan. Heat until the sugar dissolves, bring to a boil, and continue to boil, swirling the saucepan occasionally, until the syrup is caramelized and amber in color.
4. Immediately remove the saucepan from the heat, add the diced butter (do this carefully as the caramel will foam up and spit) and 1 pinch of salt, stirring until smooth. Pour the caramel into the cake pan and tilt from side to side to coat the base evenly.
5. Starting in the center, arrange the citrus slices over the warm caramel in overlapping concentric circles. Set aside.
6. In a large bowl, cream the remaining 1 stick plus 1 tsp (4 oz./120 g) butter together with the remaining ⅓ cup (2½ oz./70 g) superfine sugar and the granulated sugar. Stir in the eggs, followed by the vanilla extract.
7. In another large bowl, combine the flour, baking powder, baking soda, 1 pinch of salt, and cinnamon. Stir half of the flour mixture into the butter-sugar mixture, then stir in the yogurt. Add the remaining dry mixture and, using an immersion blender, blend until smooth. Pour the batter over the fruit in the cake pan and bake for 35–40 minutes, until the tip of a pointed knife inserted into the center comes out clean.
8. Let the cake cool for about 10 minutes in the pan, then turn it out onto a serving plate. Serve warm or at room temperature with a scoop of the ice cream of your choice (my favorite is cinnamon).

BLOOD ORANGE AND CARDAMOM CAKE

Serves 8

ACTIVE TIME
15 minutes

COOKING TIME
35 minutes

RESTING TIME
30 minutes

INGREDIENTS

FOR THE CAKE
2 blood oranges, preferably
    organic
1 stick plus 1 tsp (4 oz./120 g)
    unsalted butter, softened, plus
    more for greasing the pan
½ cup (3½ oz./100 g) superfine
    sugar
½ cup plus 1 tbsp (4 oz./110 g)
    granulated sugar
2 eggs
1⅔ cups (7 oz./200 g) all-purpose
    flour
1 pinch salt
2 tsp baking powder
½ tsp baking soda
2 tsp ground cardamom
1⅓ cups (300 ml) crème fraîche
A few edible flowers (optional)

FOR THE GLAZE
Juice of 1 blood orange
2 cups (8¾ oz./250 g)
    confectioners' sugar
Fresh or candied blood orange
    slices and edible flowers,
    for garnish (optional)

1. Preheat the oven to 350°F (180°C/Gas Mark 4) and grease an 11-inch (28-cm) round cake pan with butter. Finely grate the zest of both blood oranges and juice one of them.

2. In a large bowl, combine the butter, superfine sugar, granulated sugar, and blood orange zest until pale and creamy. Beat in the eggs one at a time, then stir in the blood orange juice. In another bowl, combine half of the flour with the salt, baking powder, baking soda, and cardamom.

3. Stir two-thirds of the flour-cardamom mixture into the egg-butter mixture, followed by half of the crème fraîche. Gently incorporate the remaining plain flour and the rest of the crème fraîche. Finally, fold in the remaining third of the flour-cardamom mixture.

4. Pour the batter into the cake pan and bake for 35 minutes—the tip of a pointed knife inserted into the center should come out clean. If the cake is not done, bake it for another 10 minutes or so. Remove the cake from the oven and let it cool in the pan for 30 minutes, before turning it out onto a wire rack to cool completely.

5. To make the glaze, whisk the blood orange juice and confectioners' sugar together. The glaze should be thick enough to coat the top of the cake and run down the sides, so add more confectioners' sugar as needed. Pour the glaze evenly over the cake and chill briefly in the refrigerator if you are not serving it right away.

6. If you like, decorate the cake with a few blood orange slices (fresh or candied) and some edible flowers.

BERRY PAVLOVA

Serves 6

ACTIVE TIME
15 minutes

COOKING TIME
1 hour 15 minutes

RESTING TIME
25 minutes

INGREDIENTS

FOR THE MERINGUE

6 egg whites, at room temperature
1⅔ cups (12 oz./340 g) superfine sugar
1½ tsp distilled white vinegar
1½ tbsp cornstarch
3 handfuls shelled toasted pistachios, roughly
   chopped

FOR THE TOPPING

Assorted berries (raspberries, strawberries,
   blackberries, blueberries, currants, etc.)
Vanilla-flavored whipped cream (optional)
A few fresh mint leaves (optional), to garnish

1. To make the meringue, preheat the oven to 230°F (115°C/Gas Mark ¼) and line a baking sheet with parchment paper.
2. Beat the egg whites until they begin to hold firm peaks. Very gradually add the sugar, beating constantly.
3. Still beating, add the vinegar, then beat in the cornstarch. Continue beating until the meringue holds firm, glossy peaks.
4. Using a spatula, gently transfer half of the meringue to the baking sheet and spread it into a circle or rectangle. Sprinkle with half of the pistachios and top with the remaining meringue. Scatter the remaining pistachios over the surface.
5. Bake for 1 hour 15 minutes, then turn off the heat and leave the oven door slightly ajar. Let the meringue cool for 20–25 minutes in the oven. You can then keep the meringue in the refrigerator if you will not be serving it right away—just be sure to take it out 45 minutes before serving.
6. To prepare the topping, wash and prepare the berries (hull any that need hulling and cut any larger berries into pieces, if you like). Set the meringue on a serving plate and top it with a thick layer of whipped cream, if using. Arrange the fruit attractively on top and garnish with a few mint leaves, if using.

SUMMER FRUIT SALAD

Serves 5

ACTIVE TIME
15 minutes

CHILLING TIME
20 minutes

INGREDIENTS
5 apricots
Scant 2 cups (9 oz./250 g) strawberries
Scant 1 cup (4½ oz./125 g) blackberries
1¼ cups (4½ oz./125 g) blueberries
1 cup (4½ oz./125 g) raspberries
3½ tbsp (50 ml) orange blossom water
1 tbsp honey
½ bunch fresh mint
A few edible flowers, such as borage,
    dill flowers, etc.

1. Wash all of the fruit, then cut the apricots, strawberries, blackberries, and blueberries (if they are large) into small pieces, setting aside a few whole berries.
2. In a large bowl, gently combine the cut fruit with the raspberries (left whole).
3. Chop the leaves of the mint sprigs, reserving a few whole leaves for garnish. In a small bowl, combine half of the orange blossom water and about half of the chopped mint leaves with the honey (experiment with different proportions to find your perfect blend). Add to the fruit and gently stir to combine. Place in the refrigerator for about 20 minutes to allow the flavors to develop.
4. To serve, place the fruit salad in ramekins or small bowls. Top with the remaining whole berries, whole mint leaves, and edible flowers. Combine the remaining orange blossom water with the rest of the chopped mint leaves and serve on the side for drizzling.

KITCHEN NOTES: This recipe is highly adaptable, so feel free to use different fruits and quantities, as it takes your fancy!

STRAWBERRY MERINGUE SALAD WITH HAZELNUTS AND MINT

Serves 6–8

ACTIVE TIME
10 minutes

INGREDIENTS
2 lb. (1 kg) strawberries
Juice of 1 orange, preferably organic
1 tbsp lemon juice, preferably organic
2 tbsp orange blossom water
2 tbsp superfine sugar
Generous ½ cup (3 oz./80 g) toasted shelled
   hazelnuts
5 oz. (150 g) plain meringue
Leaves of 4 sprigs fresh mint, chopped
Fine julienne of lemon zest, preferably organic
   (optional)

1. Wash, hull, and quarter the strawberries and place in a shallow serving bowl.
2. In a bowl, combine the orange juice, lemon juice, orange blossom water, and sugar. Stir until the sugar dissolves, then pour over the strawberries.
3. Chop the hazelnuts, break the meringue up into small pieces using your hands, and add to the strawberries. Stir gently to combine.
4. Sprinkle with the chopped mint leaves and lemon zest, if using. Serve chilled.

PEACH AND ROSEMARY TARTLETS

Serves 6–8

ACTIVE TIME
15 minutes

CHILLING TIME
40 minutes

COOKING TIME
25 minutes

INGREDIENTS
1 egg yolk
½ cup (3½ oz./100 g) granulated or superfine
    sugar
3½ tbsp (50 ml) water or milk
2 cups (9 oz./250 g) all-purpose flour
1 pinch fleur de sel
1 stick plus 2 tsp (4½ oz./125 g) unsalted butter,
    well chilled and diced
Leaves of 2 sprigs fresh rosemary, finely
    chopped
4 tbsp liquid honey, divided
3 yellow peaches
A few small sprigs rosemary with flowers,
    to garnish

1. In a bowl, whisk the egg yolk and sugar together, then whisk in the water or milk.
2. Combine the flour and salt in a large bowl. Add the butter and rub it in with your fingertips until coarse crumbs form. Work in the egg yolk-sugar mixture and chopped rosemary leaves, until the dough just comes together in a ball. Shape into a ball, flatten the top, cover with plastic wrap, and let rest in the refrigerator for 30 minutes.
3. Preheat the oven to 350°F (180°C/Gas Mark 4). Roll the dough into a rectangle with a thickness of about ¼ inch (6 mm); cut into 6 or 8 squares. Divide 2 tablespoons of the honey between the pastry squares, spooning a little into the center of each.
4. Peel the peaches with a sharp paring knife. Pit and cut the peach flesh into pieces, and place over the honey. Fold in the corners of each dough square toward the center, press down lightly to fix in place, and chill in the refrigerator for 10 minutes.
5. Bake for 25 minutes, until the crust is lightly golden. Just before serving, drizzle the remaining honey over the tartlets and decorate with the rosemary sprigs and flowers.

ROASTED SUMMER FRUIT

Serves 5

ACTIVE TIME
15 minutes

COOKING TIME
30 minutes

INGREDIENTS
3 yellow peaches
3 white peaches
4 nectarines
⅔ cup (150 ml) orange blossom water
1 cup (4½ oz./125 g) raspberries
1 handful roughly chopped pistachios
Vanilla ice cream, for serving

1. Preheat the oven to 350°F (180°C/Gas Mark 4).
2. Wash, pit, and slice the peaches and nectarines, leaving the skin on.
3. Place in a baking dish, drizzle with the orange blossom water, and bake for 25–30 minutes, until the peaches are very tender and slightly caramelized around the edges.
4. Just before serving (preferably while warm), scatter the raspberries over the peaches and top with several scoops of vanilla ice cream. Sprinkle with the pistachios and serve.

NECTARINE AND BLUEBERRY SKILLET CAKE

Serves 6

ACTIVE TIME
10 minutes

COOKING TIME
45 minutes

INGREDIENTS
1⅔ cups (7 oz./200 g) all-purpose flour
¾ cup (2 oz./60 g) almond meal
1 tsp baking powder
1 pinch baking soda
1 pinch fleur de sel
7 tbsp (4 oz./110 g) unsalted butter, softened,
   plus more for greasing the pan
¾ cup (5 oz./150 g) granulated sugar, plus more
   for serving
2 eggs
1 tsp pure vanilla extract
⅔ cup (150 ml) crème fraîche
About 2½ cups (9 oz./250 g) blueberries,
   divided
4 nectarines

1. Preheat the oven to 350°F (180°C/Gas Mark 4) and grease an ovenproof skillet with butter.
2. In a large bowl, combine the flour, almond meal, baking powder, baking soda and fleur de sel.
3. In another large bowl, combine the butter and sugar until pale and creamy, then stir in the eggs and vanilla extract. Add the flour mixture in two or three stages, alternating with the crème fraîche.
4. Gently fold 1¼ cups (4½ oz./125 g) of the blueberries into the batter, then pour half of the batter into the prepared skillet.
5. Peel and thinly slice 1 nectarine and distribute evenly over the batter in the skillet. Cover with the remaining batter.
6. Slice the remaining nectarines, leaving the skin on, and arrange the slices on top of the batter, overlapping them in concentric circles. Bake for 45 minutes, until the cake is golden brown and the tip of a pointed knife inserted into the center comes out clean.
7. Arrange the remaining blueberries on top of the cake and sprinkle with a little granulated sugar. Serve warm or at room temperature.

ROASTED NECTARINES WITH CARDAMOM-PECAN GRANOLA

Serves 6

ACTIVE TIME
10 minutes

COOKING TIME
15 minutes

INGREDIENTS
3 nectarines
1 tub frozen yogurt, for serving

FOR THE GRANOLA
1¾ cups (5 oz./150 g) rolled oats
2 tsp ground cinnamon
2 tsp ground cardamom
¾ cup (3 oz./80 g) unsweetened shredded
   coconut
Scant 1 cup (3 oz./80 g) sliced almonds
Generous ½ cup (2 oz./60 g) pecan halves,
   roughly chopped
¼ cup (60 ml) maple syrup
¼ cup (2 oz./60 g) solid coconut oil,
   melted and cooled
1 tsp pure vanilla extract

1. Preheat the oven to 375°F (190°C/Gas Mark 5).
2. To prepare the granola, combine the oats, cinnamon, cardamom, coconut, almonds, and pecans in a large bowl, until well blended.
3. In a small bowl, whisk the maple syrup and coconut oil together; whisk in the vanilla extract. Pour over the oat mixture and stir to coat evenly.
4. Wash the nectarines and cut them in half, removing the pits.
5. Place the nectarines cut side down at one end of a rimmed baking sheet. Distribute the granola in an even layer across the other end of the baking sheet—press down on the granola to pack it down slightly. Bake for 15 minutes, stirring the granola with a wooden spoon halfway through the cooking time. The granola should be lightly toasted and the nectarines tender and a little caramelized around the edges.
6. You can serve this dessert family style or individually. For a family style presentation, place all of the nectarine halves cut side up on a large serving plate and sprinkle the granola over them; top with scoops of frozen yogurt. For individual servings, place a half-nectarine with the cut side up on each plate, sprinkle with granola, and finish with a scoop of frozen yogurt. In either case, serve right away!

APRICOT-THYME GALETTE

Serves 5–6

ACTIVE TIME
10 minutes

CHILLING TIME
30 minutes

COOKING TIME
45 minutes

INGREDIENTS
1 egg yolk
Scant ⅔ cup (4 oz./120 g) granulated sugar,
 divided
3½ tbsp (50 ml) water or milk
2 cups (9 oz./250 g) all-purpose flour
1 pinch fleur de sel
1 stick plus 2 tsp (4½ oz./125 g) unsalted butter,
 well chilled and diced
4 tbsp mirabelle plum jam
5 sprigs fresh thyme (2 with flowers,
 if possible, to garnish)

1. In a bowl, whisk the egg yolk and a scant ½ cup (3 oz./80 g) of the sugar together, then whisk in the water or milk.
2. Combine the flour and salt in a large bowl. Add the butter and rub it in with your fingertips until coarse crumbs form.
3. Work in the egg yolk-sugar mixture, until the dough just comes together in a ball. Shape into a round, flatten the top, cover with plastic wrap, and let rest in the refrigerator for 20 minutes.
4. Preheat the oven to 350°F (180°C/Gas Mark 4). Roll the dough into an approximately 12-inch (30-cm) round and set it on a baking sheet. Spread the jam over the dough in an even layer.
5. Wash the apricots, cut them in two, and remove the pits. Place the apricot halves in a large bowl and sprinkle with 1 generous tablespoon (20 g) of the sugar and the leaves of 3 thyme sprigs; stir gently to combine. Arrange the apricots over the dough with the cut side down, leaving a border of 2–2¾ inches (5–7 cm). Fold the dough border over the fruit, pressing it down lightly, and sprinkle with the remaining sugar. Chill in the refrigerator for about 10 minutes.
6. Bake for 40–45 minutes, until the crust is deeply golden. Garnish with the remaining thyme sprigs and serve warm.

PEACH SOUP

Serves 5–6

ACTIVE TIME
15 minutes

COOKING TIME
20 minutes

RESTING TIME
30 minutes

INGREDIENTS
6 white peaches (not too ripe)
Juice of 1 lemon, preferably organic
1⅔ cups (400 ml) water
Generous ¾ cup (190 ml) maple syrup
4 sprigs fresh lemon verbena, divided
Speculoos cookies, for serving (optional)

1. Fill a large saucepan with water and bring to a boil. Meanwhile, fill a large bowl with ice water. Carefully lower the whole peaches into the boiling water and blanch for 2 minutes, then immediately plunge them into the ice water. Leave for 1–2 minutes and drain.
2. Carefully peel the peaches and cut them into ⅓–¾-inch (1–2-cm) slices. Place in a large bowl, coat with the lemon juice, and set aside.
3. In a saucepan, combine the water and maple syrup; add 3 of the lemon verbena sprigs. Bring to a boil, reduce the heat, and let simmer for about 15 minutes to reduce. Remove from the heat, take out the lemon verbena, and let cool completely. Pour the syrup over the peaches and place in the refrigerator for 30–45 minutes.
4. Just before serving, scatter the leaves of the remaining lemon verbena sprig over the soup. Serve well chilled with speculoos cookies on the side if you like—the flavors pair beautifully!

LILY'S* CRÈME CARAMEL

Serves 6

ACTIVE TIME
15 minutes

COOKING TIME
50 minutes

INGREDIENTS
1 cup (7 oz./200 g) superfine sugar, divided
2 tbsp water
1 tsp lemon juice, preferably organic
6 eggs
4 cups (1 L) milk
1 tsp cardamom pods (about 10)
1 vanilla bean, split lengthwise and seeds
    scraped

1. Combine half of the sugar with the water and lemon juice in a saucepan. Cook over low heat, stirring constantly with a wooden spoon until the sugar dissolves and the syrup is clear, and then boil until it caramelizes.
2. Immediately pour the caramel into a 10-inch (26-cm) round ceramic baking dish, cake pan, or silicone mold. Swirl to coat the base of the dish, pan, or mold evenly and set aside.
3. Preheat the oven to 325°F (160°C/Gas Mark 3). In a large bowl, whisk the eggs, then whisk in the remaining sugar.
4. Place the milk in a saucepan with the cardamom pods and vanilla seeds; stir to combine. Bring to a simmer and remove from the heat.
5. Let the milk cool for 5 minutes, then slowly pour it into the egg-sugar mixture, whisking constantly. Pour over the caramel in the baking dish, pan, or mold.
6. Place in a large baking dish with enough water to come halfway up the sides of the round dish, pan, or mold. Bake for 50 minutes, until the custard is just set.
7. Remove the pan from the hot water bath and delicately run a knife along the edges to release the custard. Carefully turn out onto a rimmed serving plate and leave to cool. Serve well chilled.

* Lily is my maternal grandmother.

MAPLE-ROASTED APPLES AND PEARS

Serves 6

ACTIVE TIME
7 minutes

COOKING TIME
30 minutes

INGREDIENTS
3 large cooking apples (such as Belle de
  Boskoop), preferably organic
3 pears (such as Bosc or Anjou), preferably
  organic
1 tsp quatre-épices spice mix
Maple syrup
3 tbsp granola (see recipe p. 218)
2 tbsp shredded coconut
Chocolate chips (optional)
Vanilla ice cream, for serving

1. Preheat the oven to 350°F (180°C/Gas Mark 4) and line a baking sheet with parchment
   paper.
2. Wash the apples and pears, and cut them in half lengthwise. Use a teaspoon or melon
   baller to scoop out the cores and seeds, and make small hollows in the centers.
3. Slice off a little of the rounded part of each pear and apple half, to make a more stable
   base.
4. Place the apples and pears on the baking sheet with the cored side facing up.
5. Dust the fruit with the quatre-épices, then drizzle a little maple syrup into each hollow.
   Bake for 30 minutes, until the fruit is tender but not falling apart, and the tops are
   lightly browned.
6. Remove from the oven and sprinkle with the granola, coconut, and chocolate chips, if
   using. Serve immediately with vanilla ice cream.

APPLE CINNAMON GALETTE

Serves 4–6

ACTIVE TIME
10 minutes

CHILLING TIME
30 minutes

COOKING TIME
45 minutes

INGREDIENTS
1 egg yolk
½ cup (3½ oz./100 g) light brown sugar
3½ tbsp (50 ml) water or milk
2 cups (9 oz./250 g) all-purpose flour
1 pinch kosher salt
2 tbsp ground cinnamon
1 stick plus 2 tsp (4½ oz./125 g) unsalted butter,
   well chilled and diced
4 apples, such as Elstar, Royal Gala, or Pink Lady
Vanilla or hazelnut ice cream, for serving

1. In a bowl, whisk together the egg yolk and a scant ½ cup (3 oz./80 g) of the brown sugar. Whisk in the water or milk.
2. Combine the flour, salt, and cinnamon in a large bowl. Add the butter and rub it in with your fingertips, until coarse crumbs form.
3. Work in the egg yolk-sugar mixture, just until the dough comes together in a ball. Shape into a round, flatten the top, cover with plastic wrap, and let rest in the refrigerator for 30 minutes.
4. Preheat the oven to 350°F (180°C/Gas Mark 4) and roll the dough into an approximately 10-inch (26-cm) round. Place on a baking sheet.
5. Peel, core, and cut the apples into large pieces, and place on the dough, leaving a 2–2¾-inch (5–7-cm) border. Fold the dough border over the apples, pressing down lightly.
6. Sprinkle the dough and apples with the remaining sugar and bake for 40–45 minutes, until the apples are tender and the crust golden brown.
7. Serve warm with a scoop of vanilla or hazelnut ice cream.

KITCHEN NOTES: You can make this galette with a combination of apples and pears, or try spreading a little jam (mirabelle plum is an excellent choice) over the base of the galette before adding the fruit.

DECADENT PECAN CAKE

Serves 6–8

ACTIVE TIME
20 minutes

COOKING TIME
1 hour 10 minutes

INGREDIENTS
FOR THE SUGAR MIXTURE
½ cup plus 1 tbsp (4 oz./110 g) granulated sugar
¾ cup (3 oz./80 g) pecan halves, chopped, plus 10 or so for garnish
1 tbsp ground cinnamon

FOR THE CAKE
4 cups (1 lb. 2 oz./500 g) all-purpose flour
1½ tsp baking powder
1½ tsp baking soda
1 generous pinch salt
1½ cups (10½ oz./300 g) superfine sugar
1 stick plus 3 tbsp (6 oz./170 g) unsalted butter, diced and softened, plus more for greasing the pan
1½ tsp pure vanilla extract
3 eggs
1¼ cups (9¼ oz./260 g) crème fraîche

FOR THE CRUMB TOPPING
3 tbsp (1½ oz./45 g) unsalted butter, softened and diced
¾ cup plus 2 tbsp (3½ oz./100 g) all-purpose flour
½ cup plus 1 tbsp (4 oz./110 g) granulated sugar
1 tbsp ground cinnamon

FOR THE GLAZE
4 tbsp. (2 oz./60 g) unsalted butter
2 cups (14 oz./400 g) superfine sugar
1 tsp pure vanilla extract
2 tbsp milk

1. Preheat the oven to 350°F (180°C/Gas Mark 4) and grease a 9-inch (23-cm) Bundt pan.
2. To make the sugar mixture, combine the sugar, chopped pecans, and cinnamon in a small bowl. Set aside.
3. Combine the flour, baking powder, baking soda, and salt in a large bowl. In another large bowl, whisk together the sugar, butter, vanilla extract, and eggs for 2–3 minutes. Gradually fold in the flour mixture, followed by the crème fraîche.
4. Pour one-third of the batter into the prepared mold and sprinkle with one-third of the sugar mixture. Repeat twice. Bake the cake for 1 hour, until the tip of a pointed knife inserted into it comes out clean. Keep the oven on for the crumb topping. Let the cake cool for about 10 minutes in the pan, then turn it out onto a cooling rack and let cool completely.
5. To make the crumb topping, rub the butter, flour, sugar, and cinnamon together in a bowl using your fingertips, until crumbly. Spread across a rimmed baking sheet and bake for 7–8 minutes, until lightly toasted.
6. To make the glaze, melt the butter in a small saucepan over low heat. Cook, whisking frequently until lightly browned. Remove from the heat and whisk in the sugar and vanilla extract, followed by the milk, 1 tablespoon at a time. Whisk until smooth. Pour the glaze over the cake and sprinkle with the crumb topping. Garnish with the pecan halves and serve with your favorite coffee or tea.

CHOCOLATE-PECAN BALLS

Makes about 30

ACTIVE TIME
30 minutes

COOKING TIME
15 minutes

CHILLING TIME
1 hour

INGREDIENTS
1⅔ cups (5¾ oz./160 g) pecan halves, divided
8 oz. (230 g) vanilla cream-filled wafer cookies
   (*gaufrettes à la vanille*)
8 oz. (225 g) dark chocolate
½ cup (120 ml) heavy cream
¼ cup (60 ml) corn syrup
2 tsp ground cinnamon
⅓ cup (80 ml) bourbon
1 oz. (30 g) shelled hazelnuts
1 oz. (30 g) walnut halves
Lemon curd, for serving (optional)

1. Finely chop 1⅓ cups (4½ oz./130 g) of the pecan halves, crush the wafer cookies, and stir both together in a large bowl until evenly combined.
2. Chop or break the chocolate into pieces and place in a large heatproof bowl.
3. In a saucepan over medium heat, bring the heavy cream and corn syrup to a simmer, stirring constantly. Pour immediately over the chocolate and stir until smooth. Let cool for a few minutes, then stir in the cinnamon and bourbon.
4. Pour the chocolate mixture over the pecan-wafer cookie mixture and stir until the chocolate is evenly distributed. Place the bowl in the refrigerator for at least 1 hour.
5. Meanwhile, line an airtight storage container with parchment paper. Finely chop the remaining pecans, hazelnuts, and walnuts; place them in a shallow bowl and toss to combine well.
6. Remove the chocolate-wafer mixture from the refrigerator and shape a tablespoon of the mixture into a small ball; repeat until all of the mixture has been used. Roll each ball in the nut mixture to coat completely, then place in the parchment-lined storage container. Keep the balls covered tightly in the refrigerator or freezer until serving. Serve with lemon curd, if you wish, and your favorite coffee, or bourbon!

INSPIRATION FOR
YOUR TABLE

APPLE CANDLE HOLDERS

5 apples (flat-bottomed and stable)
1 sharp knife
1 cutting board
5 long candles or tea lights

In the top of each apple, cut a hole with the same diameter as that of your candles. If you are using long candles, make the hole at least 1½ inches (4 cm) deep; for tea lights, make the hole just deep enough to fit the tea lights inside. Nestle the candles into the holes of these ephemeral candle holders and use to decorate your table. For winter holiday celebrations, tie plaid or gold-colored ribbons around the apples for a festive touch.

GLASS BOTTLE CANDLE HOLDERS
WITH FRESH HERBS

5–7 repurposed clear glass bottles (such as juice, wine, or water bottles)
A few fresh herb sprigs (rosemary, oregano, sage, thyme, mint, etc.)
3–4 long candles

Thoroughly remove the labels from the bottles.

Place 1 or 2 herb sprigs in each bottle and fill with water.

Place the candles in some of the bottles and arrange
all of the bottles—both with and without candles—
on your table or buffet.

PINEAPPLE VASE

1 pineapple (flat-bottomed and stable)
1 cutting board
1 large knife
1 spoon
1 glass
Flowers and greenery of your choice

Cut off the top of the pineapple. Using the knife and spoon,
remove enough of the fruit to make room for the glass.
Save the fruit for juice or a fruit salad!

Place the glass in the hole and fill it with water.
Arrange the flowers and greenery into a lovely bouquet
to set inside your pineapple vase.

SEASONAL
TABLE RUNNER

Fresh eucalyptus stems with leaves
4 grapefruit, halved crosswise
4 Meyer lemons, halved crosswise
10 or so small lemons
15 or so small limes

Arrange the eucalyptus stems in a line down
the center of your table, over the tablecloth.

Position the fruits next to the eucalyptus stems to create
an elegant design. Experiment with different groupings as you go and have fun!

You can easily adapt the elements of this natural
table runner according to the season.

FROZEN FRUIT AND FLOWER GLASS OR CARAFE

1 plastic bottle (a little wider than the glass or carafe)
1 glass or carafe
1 cutting board and 1 knife
1 medium-sized fruit (such as a lemon or orange), sliced,
or small fruit (blueberries, blackberries, etc.)
1 pair of scissors
Assorted small flowers of your choice

Cut off the top part of the plastic bottle to make a mold for the frozen fruit and flower decoration. The mold should be shorter than the glass or carafe you are using. Place the glass or carafe inside the base of the plastic bottle.

Arrange the fruit slices or small fruits between the glass or carafe and the plastic bottle; add small flowers here and there. The fruit and flowers should fit snugly in the space between the plastic and glass.

Pour water over the flowers and fruit in the plastic base and place in the freezer for at least 4 hours. Just before using, cut and remove the plastic.

This is a great way to keep drinks cold in the warmer months!

SHELL PLACE CARDS

An assortment of shells found on the beach
A gold permanent marker

Thoroughly wash the shells in hot, soapy water to remove any sand
and residual salt, then dry them.

Using the marker, write the names of your guests on the shells.

Feel free to complement the shells with any other treasures
found on the seashore (driftwood, sea glass, pebbles, etc.).

AVOCADO DYE

Makes enough to dye 1 small fabric item (such as a napkin)
3 avocados
1 saucepan
1 bowl or container
1 small fabric item made of natural fibers

Cut the avocados in two and scoop out all of the flesh (use it for guacamole
or avocado toast). Meticulously clean the avocado peels and pits,
then cut the peels into pieces. Place the peels and pits in a pan filled
with enough water to cover your fabric and bring to a boil.
Reduce the heat and simmer for at least 30 minutes, until the water has turned
a deep maroon shade. Strain the liquid into the bowl or container.
Thoroughly wet the fabric item with water, then wring it out and submerge
it in the dye. Leave it until you are satisfied with the color, then rinse and let dry.
When washing, use the cold wash setting (up to 86°F/30°C) and line-dry in the shade.

This is an excellent way to customize napkins, tablecloths, or aprons. Try tying up the fabric
with rubber bands or string before placing it in the dye for a lovely tie-dye effect!

INDEX OF RECIPES

INDEX OF MAIN INGREDIENTS

ACKNOWLEDGMENTS

I wish to express my heartfelt thanks
to all of the wonderful "ingredients,"
without whom this joyful feast
would not have been possible:

Christophe Roué
Françoise & Jacques Brion
Germain Brion

Florence Lécuyer
Flavia Mazelin
Clélia Ozier-Lafontaine
Kate Mascaro
Helen Adedotun

Charlotte Altschul
Florian Bourienne
Elsa Bennett & Hippolyte Dard
Patrick Flamand
Ines de la Fressange & Sophie Gachet
Danièle Gerkens
Julie de Lassus Saint-Geniès
Jeanne Laville
Marie Lichtenberg
Maria Paula Ordonez
Katell Pouliquen
Emilie & Aymeric Pourbaix

My friends, my first-class tasters,
and all those who have shared
the best of times with us in the kitchen
and around the table.

The press, which has supported me
enormously since I launched
Miss Maggie's Kitchen.

Everyone who has followed me
along the way, whether it be since
the early days or more recently.

And all of the exquisite artisans
and brands featured in this book:

A Place by the Lake
Blanche Patine
Le Creuset
Flowered By - Thierry Féret
Lacanche
Maison de Vacances
Maison Margaret
Marion Graux Poterie
Opinel
La Soufflerie
Lucien Tourtoulou - Mériguet-Carrère
Vaisselle Vintage
Villa Gypsy